THORN
COOKERY
BOOK

Introdu

D1099948

This recipe book has be
Economics Department   ...... assist you in
achieving the very best from your new cooker. It
will enable you to prepare meals and dishes to
delight the people for whom you cook and of
which you will be justly proud.

If you are new to electric cooking, we do
recommend that you consult the operating
instructions supplied with your cooker. These
instructions tell you how simple the cooker is to
operate and how to keep it in tip top condition.
If you follow these instructions you can rely on
your cooker to give you years of trouble-free and
excellent service.

Please remember that Thorn are genuinely
interested in you the purchaser. Our staff,
whether Home Economists, Sales or Service will
always be pleased to give advice that will help
you to get the maximum satisfaction from your
cooker.

THORN DOMESTIC APPLIANCES (ELECTRICAL) LTD.
New Lane, Havant, Hants. PO9 2NH   Telephone: 0705 486400

Contents

Notes on the Use of this Book

1 The quantities for recipes in this book are given in metric and imperial measurement. Exact metric conversions would be difficult to work out, therefore metric equivalents have been used. Conversion tables are given on page IX

2 Weigh and measure as accurately as possible. Variation in quantity or measurement may mean adjustments in cooking time and temperature. Do not mix metric and imperial weights in one recipe as all measurements are proportionate.

3 Plain flour should be used unless otherwise stated.

4 Standard or size 4 eggs should be used unless otherwise stated.

5 Use B.S.I. measuring spoons. All spoon measures are level unless otherwise stated.

6 Collect all ingredients and equipment required before commencing work and warm serving dishes where required.

7 If soft tub or table margarines are used for baking then they must be used straight from the refrigerator and not over-creamed. These types of margarine oil very quickly resulting in heavy cakes or cause an initial rise, then sink in the middle. The use of lower oven temperatures for a longer time will prevent soft margarines oiling too quickly during cooking and will ensure a more even rise. Alternatively you may like to try the one stage methods and recipes recommended by the margarine manufacturers.

8 Where an asterisk * is shown in some recipes, this denotes that half quantities should be used for cooking in a second oven or table cooker.

9 The recipes in this book give comparisons in cooking temperatures between conventional main ovens, second ovens and fan ovens.

10 The recipes in this book make reference to shelf positions for conventional main oven at the **top, middle** and **bottom.** These indicate oven areas, ie. top third, middle third and bottom third. For more specific shelf positions refer to the instruction leaflet supplied with your cooker. In second ovens, all cooking should be carried out on one of the lower runners (page V). When placing food in a fan oven, the shelf position is not critical (page VI).

Notes on the Use of your Cooker

Full instructions on the operation of your cooker are given in the instructions supplied. However, the following additional notes may be useful.

1 The temperatures given in this book are intended as a guide only, and it may be necessary to increase or decrease the temperature by 10°C to suit individual preferences or requirements.

2 If your cooker includes a fan oven or a second oven, you will find the notes in this book most helpful.

3 If your cooker has both a main and second oven and both are in use at the same time, you may find a slight temperature adjustment is required depending on the quantity and type of food being cooked.

4 Under certain conditions, condensation may form on the cooker during cooking. Provided that it is wiped and dried during or after cooking is complete no harm should occur to the cooker. Condensation is quite normal and forms when moisture is present e.g. during cooking. It is not necessarily caused by extremes of temperature but as a result of one or more of the following:—
(1) Quantity of food.
(2) Temperature of the food when placed in the oven.
(3) Moisture present in the food.
(4) The cooking temperature selected.
(5) Kitchen temperature.
(6) Ventilation of the kitchen.

Ideal cooking conditions are not always available but where possible, ensure foods which contain a lot of moisture e.g. casseroles, are covered. A boiling kettle produces steam, and similarly, when food gets to cooking temperature, steam is also produced which condenses onto colder surfaces.

The Second Oven

If your cooker includes a second oven, not only does it provide alternative or additional cooking space, but it can also be used as a hotcupboard or warming compartment. Various uses of the second oven compartment are given in the appropriate instruction leaflet for each model. A second oven is usually heated (unless otherwise specified) by the grill element at the top of the compartment and an element situated under the base of the compartment.

The use of the second oven may be new to you and therefore we have noted some points to assist you in its application as a cooking compartment.

Placing Food In The Oven

Due to the heating characteristics of the second oven, be careful not to place food too close to the grill element, particularly in the case of bread or larger cakes which rise up during the cooking process. In addition, do not place critical food or dishes directly onto the floor of the compartment above the lower element.

All cooking should be carried out on the shelf positioned on one of the lower runners although with most dishes, satisfactory results are obtained on the lowest runner position. Place food as centrally as possible under the grill element.

Quantities

The second oven is thermostatically controlled and is designed to cook all the dishes given in this book only on a smaller scale. Therefore it may be necessary to halve quantities for recipes or cook in two batches, depending on the type of dish to be cooked.

Lower Temperatures

When cooking in the second oven, lower temperatures are usually required compared with a conventional main oven. However, this is dependent upon the quantity of food and the shape and size of the container. Food placed in larger, shallower dishes tend to cook more quickly than if placed in deeper, narrower ones. Also it may be necessary to increase or decrease the recommended oven temperature by 10°C to allow for individual preferences and requirements.

Cooking Times

Due to the smaller cooking area, cooking times may be shorter when using the second oven compared with the conventional main oven, but this will depend on the type and quantity of the food to be cooked and the oven temperature used. Your favourite, tried and tested recipes can be cooked in the second oven selecting the food item most similar to the recipe you are using.

The Fan Oven

The hot air circulating inside a fan oven is a process which has been used in the catering industry for many years. Although domestic models have been available for about 10 years, their concept in cooking is relatively new and therefore a short explanation of their design and use may help you to adjust to all the features.

The principle of the fan oven is quite unlike a conventional one. The air inside the oven is heated by a circular electric element which is placed around a fan, situated behind the oven back panel. The fan draws air from the oven, the element around the fan heats the air which is then forced into the oven through slots at the top and bottom of the back panel. The hot air circulates continuously, immediately surrounding the food to be cooked and resulting in a fast transfer of heat into the dish. With this system of cooking food, there are many advantages.

Preheating The Oven

When cooking in the fan oven, preheating is usually unnecessary due to the fast warm up time. With some food items however, better results are obtainable if the oven is preheated first e.g. bread and yeast mixtures, some pastry dishes, scones, souffles etc.

The cooking times given do not include the additional time required when cooking from a cold oven. Allow 5–10 minutes extra time for low temperature cooking and 15–20 minutes extra time for high temperature cooking.

Lower Temperatures

The temperature at which food is cooked in a fan oven is lower than a conventional main oven and a comparison of temperatures can be seen in the recipes in this book. Your favourite recipes can still be cooked by selecting the temperature required for the dish most similar to the recipe you are using. However, obviously the cooking temperature required depends on individual preferences and requirements, and you may find it necessary to adjust the oven control dial 10°C higher or lower to allow for this.

Even Heating

Conventional ovens rely on the natural circulation of hot air in the oven and consequently do not produce *such* even heating characteristics as a fan oven. *Most* fan ovens are produced with four shelves and with the variety of runner positions allow most dishes to be cooked equally well on any shelf. The shelves should be spaced to suit the load being cooked and, of course, it is not always necessary to use all the shelves provided if cooking only one or two dishes. When only 1 dish is being cooked, it should be placed on the middle of the shelf.

If necessary, one shelf may be placed directly on the floor of the oven to give extra space when required. Although a dish may be placed directly on the floor of the oven itself, the use of the shelf does allow some air circulation under the base of the dish.

Batch Baking

The fan oven is excellent for batch baking as the uniform heating throughout ensures *more* even cooking. This means that it is possible to bake on all the shelves at the same time, ensuring that they are evenly spaced to suit the load being cooked (watch yeast doughs which swell during cooking).

When batch baking foods of the same size and type e.g. equal trays of small cakes *or* equal size Victoria Sandwich cakes, then they can be cooked together and removed from the oven at the same time. When mixing different sizes of trays or tins or types of food e.g. biscuits and cakes, then it may be necessary to remove those which are cooked first from the oven. When the oven is fully loaded using all the shelves provided, then a slight increase in cooking time may be necessary.

Automatic Cooking

In conventional ovens, dishes requiring slight differences in cooking temperature or time can be placed higher or lower in the oven making use of the slight variation in temperature from top to bottom. In a fan oven, the uniformity of the heating requires some special considerations, but overall there is no difficulty in cooking several dishes together – even dishes of different kinds – without the taste and smell of one dish being transferred to the next.

Choose foods which require approximately the same temperature and time where possible although dishes can be "slowed down" slightly by using larger containers and covering with aluminium foil or "hurried up" slightly by cooking smaller quantities or placing in smaller containers. In addition, a smaller dish can be "slowed down" by placing it on a shelf immediately below a larger item on a shelf above, thus blanking off some of the circulating hot air.

If choosing dishes to be cooked together which do require different temperatures or cooking times, then the oven temperature selected will be a compromise and it must be accepted that some dishes will cook a little more quickly than normal whilst others will cook a little more slowly.

Defrosting

Due to the fast circulating air in the fan oven, it is possible to defrost some food items using the low temperature settings on the oven temperature control.

Bread, cakes, biscuits and individual tarts or pies may be thawed unwrapped in the oven at 80/90°C. However, bread and cakes may go stale more quickly if thawed in this way.

Small cooked pastry items e.g. tarts, pies, sausage rolls and mince-pies can be heated through without thawing them first. Place into a cold oven set at 190/200°C for 20–40 minutes depending on quantity, size and the required serving temperature.

A medium size casserole or stew may be reheated without thawing first. Place into a cold oven set at 180/190°C for $1\frac{3}{4}$–$2\frac{1}{4}$ hours, depending on the size and shape of the container. It will be necessary to stir or break up the contents during the heating process.

A $1\frac{1}{2}$kg (3lb) oven ready chicken may be thawed at 80/90°C in $1\frac{1}{2}$ hours. Place the chicken in a roasting bag and always cook the chicken immediately after thawing.

Commercially prepared frozen foods may be cooked as directed on the packet but allow 25% less cooking time.

Cleaner Cooking

With no radiant elements in the fan oven to cause hot spots, splashings are kept to a minimum. In some fan ovens, stay clean panels are fitted which means no manual cleaning is necessary at all (see your operating instructions). However, always use the meat tin trivet (where provided) to minimise splatterings during roasting and burn off the stay clean liners afterwards if necessary as advised in the operating instructions.

Oven Temperatures

The oven control on your cooker is now scaled in degrees Celsius, which is abbreviated to °C. The temperatures given in the recipes are shown in °C and it will be helpful to remember that the metric cooking temperatures are approximately one half of the Fahrenheit Scale.

'Cool'
'Slow'

'Moderate'

'Fairly hot'

'Hot'

'Very hot'

Table of temperature equivalents for oven thermostat markings.

Fahrenheit Scale	Celsius Scale	Gas Reg.
175	80	
200	**100**	
225	110	
250	120	$\frac{1}{2}$
275	140	1
300	**150**	2
325	160	3
350	180	4
375	190	5
400	**200**	6
425	220	7
450	230	8
475	240	9
500	**260**	
525	270	

Frying Temperatures

First frying of potatoes.

Croquettes, rissoles, large fillets fish, fruit fritters, cutlets,

Second frying of potatoes, small fritters, croutons etc.

300	150
340	170
350	175
360	180
370	190
380	195
390	200

Note: When deep fat frying, for safety purposes, fill pan only one third full of oil or fat.
Do not use a lid when deep fat frying.

Measurement of Ingredients

Metric equivalents used	Imperial	Exact conversions
Mass (weight)		
15grams	$\frac{1}{2}$oz	14.17grams
25g	1oz	28.35g
50g	2oz	56.70g
100g	4oz	113.40g
200g	8oz	226.80g
300g	12oz	340.20g
400g	1lb	453.60g
1kilo	2lb	907.20g
Capacity (liquid measures)		
25millilitres	1fl. oz	28.35millilitres
50ml	2fl. oz	56.70ml
125ml	5fl. oz	141.75ml
250ml	$\frac{1}{2}$pt	283.50ml
375ml	$\frac{3}{4}$pt	425.25ml
500ml	1pt	567.00ml
1litre	$1\frac{3}{4}$pt	992.25ml
Length		
2.5centimetres	1in.	2.54centimetres
15cm	6in.	15.20cm
20cm	8in.	20.30cm
25millimetres	1in.	25.40millimetres
150mm	6in	152.40mm
200mm	8in.	203.20mm

Appetisers & Savouries

In this section we have included some hors d'oeuvres and starters which may be served before the main course. If the main course is a hot one, start the meal with a cold, light hors d'oeuvre, but if the meal is cold, a hot or more satisfying starter may precede it. The recipes given for 'savouries' may be used either as a finish to a formal dinner, or as party snacks.

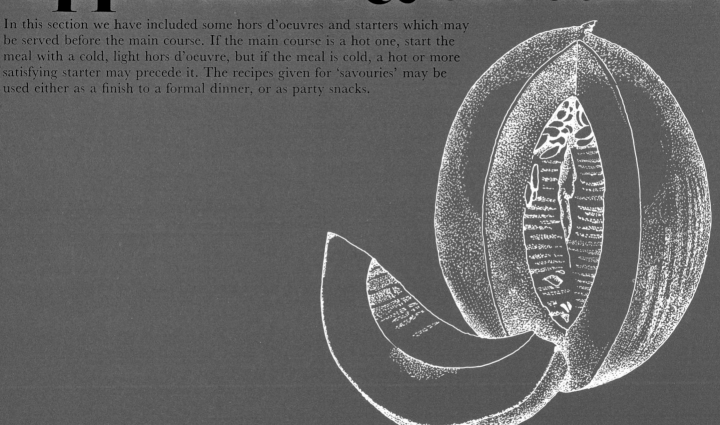

Hors-d'oeuvres

Hors d'oeuvres may be served as the first course of a meal. A good selection of cold meats, vegetables and fish served in separate small dishes are prepared so that each person can make a personal selection.

Mixed Hors-d'oeuvres

Vegetables

1 Sliced tomatoes in french dressing with chopped chives.
2 Sautéd mushrooms with finely chopped onion.
3 Olives, black, green or stuffed.
4 Radishes, sliced or cut into rose shapes.
5 Cucumber, finely sliced and served with vinegar and chopped parsley.
6 Diced beetroot in vinegar.
7 Potato salad, cold boiled potatoes, diced and folded into mayonnaise.
8 Russian salad—cold cooked vegetables, diced and folded into mayonnaise.

Fish

1 Anchovies.
2 Sardines.
3 Smoked salmon.
4 Prawns or shrimps.
5 Potted shrimps in butter.
6 Cold cooked salmon.
7 Herring roll mops.
8 Smoked buckling.
9 Cold cooked smoked haddock.

Meat

1 Sliced cold sausages—salami, liver sausage etc.
2 Sliced cooked ham.
3 Sliced paté.
4 Sliced cooked chicken in a little mayonnaise.
5 Parma smoked ham.

Eggs

1 Hard boiled and sliced.
2 Hard boiled and covered with mayonnaise—paprika pepper sprinkled on top.

Egg Mayonnaise

Method

1 Cut eggs lengthways into halves.
2 Wash and shred the lettuce, dry thoroughly, place on the individual plates.
3 Place the eggs on lettuce, cut side down, cover with mayonnaise.
4 Decorate with chopped parsley or paprika pepper.

Ingredients

4 hard boiled eggs, shelled
3–4 lettuce leaves
125ml ($\frac{1}{4}$pt) mayonnaise
parsley, chopped
paprika pepper

Serves 4

Avocado Pear with Prawn or Crab

Method

1 Prepare avocado pear, halve by cutting around the stone with a sharp stainless steel knife. Separate the two halves by twisting, discard the stone.
2 Sprinkle with lemon juice to prevent browning.
3 Fill the hollow with prawns or crab bound with mayonnaise.

Ingredients

2 avocado pears
lemon juice
100g (4oz) prawns or crab, prepared
3 15ml (table) spoon mayonnaise

Serves 4

Florida Cocktail

Method

1 Remove peel from grapefruit and oranges by peeling with a sharp knife, making sure to remove all the pith.
2 Cut into either side of the segments and remove flesh in sections.
3 Place in glasses, alternate segments of grapefruit and orange. Pour over any juice from preparation and liqueur. Add sugar to taste.
4 Decorate with cherries.
5 Serve chilled.

Ingredients

2 small grapefruit
2 large oranges
orange liqueur
sugar
4 marachino cherries

Serves 4

Melon Balls

Method

1 Slice top off melon, remove seeds.
2 Scoop out flesh with a parisian cutter or 5ml (tea) spoon.
3 Place in bowl, dredge melon balls with sugar and wine, chill.
4 Either refill melon shell or serve in individual dishes.

Ingredients

1 honeydew melon
2 15ml (table) spoon caster sugar
2 15ml (table) spoon madeira or sherry

Serves 4–6

Prawn Cocktail

Method

1 Shred the lettuce finely, season and add squeeze of lemon juice. Place in glasses or dishes.
2 Mix together mayonnaise, tomato ketchup, and worcester sauce.
3 If using fresh prawns, shell and wash before using. Leave one per portion with shell for decoration.
4 Place prawns on bed of lettuce. Pour over sauce.
5 Decorate each with a prawn and slice of lemon.

Ingredients

4–8 lettuce leaves
seasoning
lemon juice
3 15ml (table) spoon mayonnaise
1 15ml (table) spoon tomato ketchup
1 15ml (table) spoon worcester sauce
100g (4oz) frozen prawns or 375ml ($\frac{3}{4}$pt) fresh prawns
lemon slices

Serves 4

Smoked Trout Paté

Method

1 Remove skin and bone from the trout and flake the fish into a basin.
2 Add lemon juice, cayenne and black pepper to taste.
3 Mash with a wooden spoon or blend until smooth.
4 Stir in the cream cheese and parsley and mix thoroughly.
5 Place into a container and leave until chilled in a refrigerator.
6 Serve with fingers of brown toast.

Ingredients

3 smoked trout
juice 1 lemon
$\frac{1}{4}$ 5ml (tea) spoon cayenne pepper
ground black pepper
75g (3oz) cream cheese
2 5ml (tea) spoon, parsley, chopped

Serves 6

Soufflé Rarebit

Method
1 Toast the bread.
2 Mix together egg yolk, 50g (2oz) grated cheese, butter and seasoning.
3 Whisk egg white until stiff and add to mixture.
4 Pour over toast, sprinkle the rest of the grated cheese over the top.
5 Place under grill to brown. Serve immediately.

Ingredients
2 slices bread
1 egg, separated
75g (3oz) cheese, grated
25g (1oz) butter
seasoning
mustard

Serves 2

Soft Roe Savoury

Method
1 Wash roes, dry well and fry gently in butter for 8–10 minutes, drain.
2 Place on freshly toasted bread, season.
3 A squeeze of lemon juice is added to give extra flavour. Decorate with a sprig of parsley.

Ingredients
12 herring roes
50g (2oz) butter
6 fingers of toast
seasoning
lemon juice
parsley

Serves 3–6

Scotch Eggs

Method
1 Shell eggs and dry.
2 Roll in seasoned flour and cover evenly with sausage meat.
3 Coat with egg and breadcrumbs.
4 Fry in hot deep fat for 8–10 minutes.
5 When cold cut into quarters and serve with salad.

Ingredients
4 eggs, hard boiled
seasoned flour
200g (8oz) sausage meat
egg, beaten
breadcrumbs

Serves 4

Liver Paté

Method

1 Grease the tin and line with the de-rinded bacon.
2 Heat oil in a frying pan. Fry liver until brown. Add pork fat and fry for a further 2 minutes.
3 Add onion and mince finely.
4 Add all the other ingredients to the minced meat and mix in well.
5 Place paté into the tin, smooth top. Cover with foil.
6 Place in a roasting tin of water. Bake.
7 Cool slightly. To press, place weights on top of paté, place in refrigerator overnight.
8 When serving turn out of tin and garnish with slices of gherkin and tomato.

Ingredients

8–10 rashers of bacon
1 15ml (table) spoon oil
400g (1lb) lambs liver, diced
50g (2oz) pork fat, diced
1 small onion, chopped
100g (4oz) pork sausage meat
40g (1½oz) white breadcrumbs
2 egg yolks
65ml (⅛pt) brandy or dry white wine
seasoning

gherkins, sliced
tomatoes, sliced

Cooking

Main oven temperature: 160°C
Time: 1–1½ hrs
Tin: 1kg (2lb) loaf tin
Shelf: middle
⎡ Second oven
  temperature: 150–160°C
  Fan oven
⎣ temperature: 150°C

Serves 8–12

Sausage Rolls

Method

1 Roll out pastry into an oblong about 25 × 50cm (10 × 20in.). Cut into two pieces lengthwise.
2 Halve sausage meat and roll each piece into a long strip 50cm (20in.) long. Place on pastry.
3 Damp edge of pastry, roll round sausage meat, sealing edges.
4 Brush with beaten egg.
5 Cut each strip into 6 equal portions. Make 2 cuts in top of each roll.
6 Place on baking tray. Bake.

Variations

2 15ml (table) spoon mixed herbs or
1 5ml (tea) spoon curry powder or   } mixed with sausage meat
25g (1oz) finely chopped onion.

Ingredients

200g (8oz) flaky or rough puff pastry (page 128)
400g (1lb) sausage meat
egg, beaten

Cooking

Main oven temperature: 230°C
Time: 25–35 mins
Tin: baking trays
Shelf: top and middle
⎡ Second oven
  temperature: 210–220°C
  Fan oven
⎣ temperature: 220°C

Makes 12

Pizza

Method

1 Divide the dough into 4, roll out and place into 4 greased 20cm (8in.) sandwich tins. Put them to rise in a warm place.
2 Cover each with alternate layers of cheese, tomato, olives and fillets of anchovies.
3 Pour over each, one 15ml (table) spoon olive oil and dot with butter. Bake and serve very hot.

Note: For a quick Pizza use cheese scone dough recipe (page 118) cook at 200–220°C 30–40 minutes.

Ingredients*

400g (1lb) bread dough (page 131)
8 tomatoes, peeled and sliced
100g (4oz) black olives, stoned
12 anchovies
200g (8oz) gouda cheese, sliced
4 15ml (table) spoon olive oil
1 5ml (tea) spoon butter

Cooking

Main oven temperature: 230°C
Time: 20–30 mins
Tins: 4 20cm (8in.)
sandwich tins
Shelf: top and middle
Second oven
temperature: 210–220°C
Fan oven
temperature: 220°C

Serves 4

Vol au Vents

Method

1 Roll out pastry to 3–6mm ($\frac{1}{8}$–$\frac{1}{4}$in.).
2 Using a 5cm (2in.) cutter, cut into rounds and place on a slightly damp baking tray.
3 Cut a smaller circle with a 12mm ($\frac{1}{2}$in.) cutter, half way through centre of each.
4 Glaze the tops with egg.
5 Bake.
6 Remove the soft centres and cool.

Fillings

250ml ($\frac{1}{2}$pt) white coating sauce.
Any of the following ingredients

150g (6oz) shrimps, prawns or other shell fish.
100g (4oz) ham, chopped, 50g (2oz) tongue, chopped.
100g (4oz) cooked chicken, chopped, 50g (2oz) ham, chopped.

Decorate with sprigs of parsley. Serve hot or cold depending on filling.

Ingredients

200g (8oz) flaky or rough puff pastry (page 128)
1 egg, beaten

Cooking

Main oven temperature: 220°C
Time: 15–20 mins
Tin: baking tray
Shelf: top and middle
Second oven
temperature: 210–220°C
Fan oven
temperature: 210°C

2 tomatoes, peeled and chopped, 75g (3oz) cheese, grated.
150g (6 oz) cooked mushrooms.
100g (4oz) tinned salmon or tuna fish and squeeze of lemon.

Makes approximately 24

Veal and Ham Patties

Method

1 Roll out pastry to a thickness 3–6mm ($\frac{1}{8}$–$\frac{1}{4}$in.) using a 6cm (2$\frac{1}{2}$in.) cutter, cut out 12 lids.
2 Roll remainder of pastry wafer thin and cut 12 bases using a 8cm (3 in.) cutter.
3 Mix together ham, veal, seasoning, thyme, parsley, lemon juice and water.
4 Line patty tins with pastry, fill with meat mixture and cover. Brush with beaten egg. Bake.

Ingredients

200g (8oz) flaky pastry (page 128)
50g (2oz) ham, chopped
150g (6oz) lean veal, chopped
seasoning
pinch of thyme
$\frac{1}{2}$ 5ml (tea) spoon parsley, chopped
1 15ml (table) spoon lemon juice
1 15ml (table) spoon water
egg, beaten

Cooking

Main oven temperature: 220°C
Time: 30–45 mins
Tin: patty tins
Shelf: top and middle
Second oven temperature: 210–220°C
Fan oven temperature: 210°C

Serves 4–6

Flans

Method

1 To bake blind, roll pastry out until it is 2.5cm (1in.) larger than tin. Place pastry in the tin, using the rolling pin to transport pastry to prevent stretching, ease in. Trim edges. Mould pastry against side of tin, with fingers. Prick base lightly, place a greaseproof paper disc in the base and cover with a few beans.
2 About 5 minutes before end of cooking time, remove paper and beans, return flan case to the oven for remainder of time to dry out the base.
3 Beat eggs, milk and seasoning together. Stir in other ingredients, place in saucepan and warm over a gentle heat.
4 When flan is cool pour in filling. Bake at once.

Basic Ingredients

150g (6oz) savoury flan pastry (page 127)
2 eggs
125ml ($\frac{1}{4}$pt) milk
seasoning

Cooking

Main oven temperature: 200°C
Time: flan bake blind 15–20 mins; filling 25–35 mins
Tin: 20cm (8in.) sandwich tin
Shelf: middle
Second oven temperature: 180–190°C
Fan oven temperature: 180–190°C

Fillings

Cheese and tomato: 100g (4oz) mature cheddar cheese, grated, pinch mustard, pinch cayenne, 2 large tomatoes, sliced.
Chicken and mushroom: 100g (4oz) cooked chicken, chopped, 50g (2oz) cooked mushrooms, sliced.
Ham and herb: 100g (4oz) ham, chopped, 1 level 5ml (tea) spoon mixed herbs, 25g (1oz) onion, finely chopped.
Salmon and celery: 200g (8oz) tinned salmon, 2 sticks celery, chopped, few drops of vinegar.
Spanish: 25g (1oz) green peppers, chopped, 25g (1oz) mushrooms, sliced, 15g ($\frac{1}{2}$oz) onions, finely chopped, 50g (2oz) cheese, grated, decorate with stuffed olives.

Serves 4–6

Baked Stuffed Tomatoes

Method

1 Cut a thin slice off the rounded end of the tomatoes and scoop out the centres leaving the shells, retain pulp.
2 Heat the oil and fry onions and garlic for a few minutes, add and fry the mushrooms, season to taste, add the crumbs and the tomato pulp.
3 Fill the tomato shells with the mixture, piling it up well, replace tops.
4 Place in a greased baking dish, sprinkle with cheese and bake.

Ingredients

4–5 large firm tomatoes
1 15ml (table) spoon oil
1–2 small onions, chopped
1 clove garlic, crushed
3–4 mushrooms, chopped
seasoning
3–4 15ml (table) spoon breadcrumbs
2 15ml (table) spoon parmesan cheese, grated

Cooking

Main oven temperature: 190°C
Time: 20–25 mins
Dish: oval ovenware
Shelf: middle
Second oven temperature: 180–190°C
Fan oven temperature: 180°C

Makes 4–5

Stuffed Tomato Salad

Method

1 Cut a slice from the stem end of each tomato, scoop out the seeds and pulp. Sprinkle insides with salt and invert to drain.
2 Mix other ingredients together with a little of sieved tomato pulp to make thick mixture.
3 Stuff the tomato shells liberally. Chill and serve on bed of lettuce.

Ingredients

10 large tomatoes
100g (4oz) cooked chicken, chopped or small tin of salmon
1 small onion, chopped
2 sticks celery, chopped
1 orange, peeled and diced
salad cream

Makes 10

Savoury Pancakes

Pouring Batter (page 74)

Method

1 Prepare a 12mm ($\frac{1}{2}$in.) thick based frying pan by melting a little butter in it and coating the base and sides. Pour off the excess butter.
2 Pour a little batter into the pan and cover the base completely.
3 Cook until golden brown underneath, turn with a palette knife. Cook second side. Use according to the recipe.

Fillings

Cottage cheese and prawn. Mix 50g (2oz) cottage cheese, 50g (2oz) prawns, seasoning, 50g (2oz) cucumber and a squeeze of lemon. Fill pancakes, serve with lemon wedges.

Beef. Cook 100g (4oz) minced beef in stock with seasoning and onion. Drain stock off and add 25g (1oz) cooked peas, a few drops of worcester sauce and few herbs. Fill pancakes. Serve with tomato sauce (page 32).

Also fillings recommended for vol au vents may be used for pancakes. Serve hot with lemon wedges.

Egg & Cheese Cookery

Eggs and cheese are invaluable for making quick snacks and when compared with other sources of protein such as meat and fish, are comparatively cheap and are available all the year round.

Methods of Cooking Eggs

Boiled

1 Cover the base of a saucepan with approximately 6mm ($\frac{1}{4}$in.) of water.
2 Place the saucepan with a tight fitting lid over the hotplate and turn the control to maximum heat.
3 When the water boils, lower the egg or eggs gently into the water with a spoon. Replace the lid and reduce the heat.
4 Simmer for 3–4 minutes for a light to firm set.
5 Cook for 10 minutes for hard boiled eggs.

Scrambled

1 Melt a knob of butter in a saucepan
2 Whisk eggs, add seasoning and 1 15ml (table) spoon milk for each egg.
3 Pour eggs into saucepan and cook over a low heat, stirring continuously until the eggs thicken.
4 Remove from heat but continue stirring until the mixture sets.
5 Serve with hot buttered toast.

Fried

1 Melt a little fat in a frying pan.
2 Break eggs one at a time into a saucer and lower them into the hot fat.
3 Cook gently, basting with the fat until the eggs are set.
4 If bacon is required, the rashers should be cooked first, and then the eggs may be fried in the hot bacon fat.

Plain Omelette

Method

1 Melt the butter in a heavy based omelette pan or frypan. Whisk the eggs, seasoning and water.
2 When the butter is hot, pour in the egg mixture and cook over a gentle heat, drawing the sides of the omelette into the centre, so that the uncooked egg runs to the sides.
3 When the egg has set, cook without stirring until the omelette is golden underneath.
4 Tilt the pan and fold one third of the omelette to the centre and then fold over the opposite third.
5 Turn the omelette out onto a warmed plate and serve immediately.

Omelette fillings   One of these fillings can be added to the centre of the omelette before folding.
40g (1½oz) cheese, grated.
2 tomatoes peeled, chopped and lightly fried.
50g (2oz) mushrooms, sliced and lightly fried.
2 rashers of bacon, without rind chopped and fried until crisp.
50g (2oz) ham, tongue, chicken, etc., chopped.
50g (2oz) shrimps or prawns.

Ingredients

allow per person :
knob of butter
2 eggs
seasoning
1 15ml (table) spoon water

Spanish Omelette

Method

1 Fry the onion in the oil, add all the vegetables and cook for a few minutes stirring.
2 Whisk the eggs and seasoning together and pour over the vegetables in the pan. Cook slowly, shaking the pan occasionally to prevent sticking.
3 When the underside is cooked and browned, place the pan under a hot grill to finish the top of the omelette.
4 Do not fold the omelette but serve on a warm plate accompanied by a green salad.

Ingredients

1 small onion, chopped
1 15ml (table) spoon olive oil
1 tomato, peeled and chopped
2 cooked potatoes, diced
2 15ml (table) spoon cooked peas
4 eggs
seasoning

Serves 2–3

Eggs a là Mornay

Method

1 Prepare the sauce and add 25g (1oz) of the grated cheese. Stir until the cheese has melted.
2 Place the eggs in an ovenware dish, reserving a few slices for garnish.
3 Pour the sauce over, then sprinkle with remaining cheese over the top. Dot with shavings of butter and brown under a hot grill.
4 Garnish with slices of egg and chopped parsley.

Ingredients

250ml (¼pt) coating sauce (page 30)
50g (2oz) cheese, grated
4 eggs, hard boiled and sliced
15g (½oz) butter
parsley, chopped

Serves 4

Stuffed Rolls

Method

1 Cut a slice from the top of the dinner rolls, scoop out the inside of the rolls. Discard half and crumb the rest.
2 Melt the butter and lightly fry the vegetables until tender but not browned. Add the crumbs, and seasoning.
3 Whisk the eggs and pour into the pan, stir until cooked.
4 Place the mixture back into the roll cases, and replace the tops.
5 Dampen the rolls with water, and place in the centre of the oven until the filling is heated and the rolls crisp.

Ingredients

6 crisp dinner rolls
25g (1oz) butter
50g (2oz) mushrooms, chopped
3 tomatoes, peeled and chopped
1 small onion, finely chopped
seasoning
3 eggs
water

Cooking

Main oven temperature: 200°C
Time: 10–15 mins
Tin: baking tray
Shelf: middle
[Second oven
temperature: 180–190°C
Fan oven
temperature: 180°C]

Makes 6

Curried Eggs

Method

1 Prepare the sauce. During the last 15 minutes of cooking time, cook rice (page 67).
2 Place the halved eggs in a warm dish and pour the sauce over.
3 Surround with rice and garnish with chopped parsley and paprika pepper.

Ingredients

250ml (½pt) curry sauce (page 33)
4 eggs, hard boiled and cut in half
100g (4oz) patna rice, freshly cooked
parsley, chopped
paprika pepper

Serves 4

Stuffed Eggs

Method

1 Cut the eggs in half lengthwise, remove the yolks and sieve them.
2 Add the mayonnaise, seasoning and butter and mix until smooth.
3 Put into a forcing bag with a star pipe and pipe back into the halved egg whites.
4 Garnish with a sprinkle of paprika pepper and sprigs of parsley.

Variations

1 5ml (tea)spoon anchovy essence
1 5ml (tea)spoon parmesan cheese, grated
1–2 5ml (tea)spoon tongue or ham, minced
One of these ingredients can be added to the yolk mixture before piping.

Ingredients

4 eggs, hard boiled
1 15ml (table) spoon mayonnaise
seasoning
25g (1oz) butter
paprika pepper
parsley

Serves 4

Egg Baked Potatoes

Method

1 Mark a circle around the top of each potato with a sharp knife and bake in the oven until soft.
2 Remove the soft potato from the centre and mash with the butter, milk, and seasoning. Place some of the mixture back into the potato cases so that they are half filled.
3 Break an egg into each potato case and return to the oven and bake until the eggs are set, 10–15 minutes.
4 Pipe or fork the remaining potato over the top, sprinkle with grated cheese and brown under the grill.

Ingredients

4 large potatoes, scrubbed
50g (2oz) butter
2 15ml (table) spoon milk
seasoning
4 eggs
100g (4oz) cheese, grated

Cooking

Main oven temperature: 200°C
Time: 1½–2 hrs
Tin: baking tray
Shelf: top/middle

Second oven temperature: 190–200°C
Fan oven temperature: 180–190°C

Serves 4

Quiche Lorraine

Method

1 Roll out the pastry and line flan ring or sandwich tin. Strengthen the sides by making a double edge.
2 Fry bacon strips gently without extra fat until just cooked but not browned, arrange the bacon over the base of the flan case.
3 Arrange cheese slices over the bacon.
4 Lightly beat the eggs and seasoning, stir in the cream and pour into the pastry case.
5 Bake towards the top of the oven until risen and golden brown. See illustration opposite page 16.

Ingredients

150g (6oz) short crust or flaky pastry (page 126, 128)
75–100g (3–4oz) lean bacon strips
75–100g (3–4oz) gruyère cheese, sliced
3 eggs
seasoning
125ml ($\frac{1}{4}$pt) single cream or top of the milk

Cooking

Main oven temperature: 200°C
Time: 30–45 mins
Tin: 18cm (7in.) flan ring, or sandwich tin
Shelf: top

Second oven temperature: 190–200°C
Fan oven temperature: 180–190°C

Serves 4

Fondue

Method

1 Rub the garlic around the inside of a fondue dish, or a heat-proof dish. Place in oven on low heat and warm the wine and lemon juice.
2 Add grated cheese to the dish stirring until the cheese and wine blend together.
3 Add the cornflour blended with the kirsch and the seasonings and continue to cook for 2–3 minutes, until the fondue thickens.
4 Serve, keeping the fondue warm over a small spirit lamp or dish warmer.

Ingredients

1 clove garlic, crushed
125ml ($\frac{1}{4}$pt) dry white wine and a squeeze of lemon juice
200g (8oz) cheese (half gruyère, half emmenthal), grated
2 5ml (tea) spoon cornflour
1 liqueur glass kirsch
a little pepper
nutmeg, grated

Serves 4

Cheese Pudding

Method

1 Grease an ovenware dish. Remove the crusts and cut the bread into cubes and place in the dish. Melt the butter and pour over the bread.

2 Lightly beat the eggs and seasonings, add the milk and mix well. Pour over the bread.

3 Sprinkle the cheese over the top and bake until risen and golden brown. Serve immediately.

Ingredients

4–6 slices white bread
25g (1oz) butter
2 eggs
seasoning
pinch dry mustard
250ml ($\frac{1}{4}$pt) milk
100g (4oz) cheese, grated

Variations

2 tomatoes, sliced,
or 40g (1$\frac{1}{2}$oz) onions, chopped,
(placed in layers with bread)

Cooking

Main oven temperature:
180–190°C
Time: 40–60 mins
Dish: 1 litre (2pt)
ovenware
Shelf: middle

Second oven
temperature: 170–180°C
Fan oven
temperature: 160–170°C

Serves 4–6

Cheese and Onion Pie

Method

1 Roll out the pastry and line pie plate.
Reserve the trimmings.

2 Simmer the onions in salted water for 5 minutes, drain well and mix with the cheese. Add seasoning and the egg, reserving a little for brushing.

3 Place the filling in the centre of the pastry. Roll out the trimmings cut strips and arrange over the pie to form a lattice design. Brush with remaining egg. Bake.

Ingredients

150g (6oz) cheese pastry (page 127)
2 onions, chopped, or 100–150g
(4–6oz) spring onions
200g (8oz) cheese, grated
seasoning
1 egg, beaten

Cooking

Main oven temperature: 200°C
Time: 30–45 mins
Tin: 23cm (9in.) pie plate
Shelf: top/middle

Second oven
temperature: 190–200°C
Fan oven
temperature: 180–190°C

Serves 4–6

Cheese Aigrettes

Method

1 Add the cheese to the choux pastry mixture, add the seasoning, beat well.

2 Heat a pan of fat and drop in 5ml (tea) spoons of the mixture. Fry until golden.

3 Drain on kitchen paper and serve.

Ingredients

50g (2oz) strong cheese, grated
basic choux pastry recipe (page 127)
seasoning
pinch cayenne pepper
deep fat for frying

Makes approximately 24

Cheese Soufflé

Method

1 Melt the butter, stir in the flour and cook for 2–3 minutes.
2 Gradually stir in the milk and bring to the boil, stirring all the time.
3 Cool slightly and add the filling.
4 Separate eggs, beat the egg yolks into the mixture one at a time and season.
5 Stiffly whisk the egg whites, fold into the mixture and put into the greased soufflé dish.
6 Bake until well risen and brown.

Variations for souffle fillings

Make basic sauce from 25g (1oz) butter, 25g (1oz) flour and 125ml (¼pt) milk:

Ham: 75g (3oz) cooked ham, finely chopped.
Fish: 75g (3oz) cooked smoked haddock, finely flaked.
Mushroom: 100g (4oz) mushrooms, chopped and lightly fried in butter.

Ingredients

25g (1oz) butter
15g (½oz) flour
125ml (¼pt) milk
75g (3oz) cheese, finely grated
3 eggs
seasoning

Cooking

Main oven temperature: 200°C
Time: 30–40 mins
Dish: 18cm (7in.)
soufflé dish
Shelf: top/middle

Second oven temperature:
180°C, 20–30 mins,
2 × 13cm (5in.) dishes
Fan oven
temperature: 170°C

Serves 4

Soups

There are two main types of soup, thin and clear or thickened. The soup chosen to precede a meal should complement the main dish, both in flavour and type. The best soups are made with good, well flavoured stocks, but if home made stocks are not available, then stock cubes may be used. Generally, white stock should be used for light coloured soups, whereas dark soups and consommé require brown stock.

In this section the number of servings has not been stated as the quantity per person will vary greatly, depending on whether the soup is to be served as one of a number of courses in a meal or as a snack. However, as a general guide allow 125–250ml ($\frac{1}{4}$–$\frac{1}{2}$pt) per person, depending when it is to be served.

White Stock

Method

1 Place bones, bouquet garni, and salt in saucepan, cover with water and bring to the boil.
2 Add prepared vegetables, place lid on pan and simmer for 2–3 hours.
3 Strain before use.

Ingredients

400g (1lb) veal bone, knuckle
bouquet garni
1 5ml (tea) spoon salt
750ml (1½pts) cold water
1 onion, chopped
1 stick celery, sliced

Brown Stock

Method

1 Brown bones in oven.
2 Place prepared bones, pieces of meat, bouquet garni, and salt into a saucepan, cover with water and bring to the boil.
3 Add prepared vegetables, place lid on pan and simmer for 2–3 hours.
4 Strain before use.

Ingredients

400g (1lb) bones, beef or veal
200g (8oz) shin of beef
bouquet garni
1 5ml (tea) spoon salt
750ml (1½pts) cold water
1 onion, chopped
1 stick celery, sliced

Bouquet Garni

Method

1 Tie the herbs together in a small square of muslin with cotton or string leaving a long end free to tie to the handle of the pan.
2 Place the bouquet garni in the pan during cooking to improve the flavour of soups and casseroles etc. Remove before serving.
3 Fresh herbs can be used if preferred.

Ingredients

Using dried herbs:
small bay leaf
pinch mixed herbs
6 peppercorns
1 clove
pinch dried parsley

Consommé

Method

1 Shred the meat, removing all fat, place in the cold stock with prepared vegetables, peppercorns, bouquet garni and salt.
2 Crush the egg shells and add with egg whites to the stock.
3 Whisk the consommé while heating until froth begins to form. Stop whisking, bring to boil. Reduce heat immediately and simmer gently for 2 hrs. Do not over boil or the consommé will cloud.
4 Strain through muslin twice, reheat and add a little sherry.

Ingredients

400g (1lb) lean beef
2¼litres (4pts) brown stock
1 onion, chopped
1 stick celery, sliced
2 carrots, sliced
12 peppercorns
bouquet garni
salt
2 egg whites and shells
sherry

Garnishes

Julienne: Cut vegetables into matchstick shapes and cook separately, add to hot consommé.
Vermicelli: Cooked and added to hot consommé.
Cold consommé: When the consommé has been made, allow to cool and then place in a refrigerator, where it will set to a jelly Beat the jellied soup and serve in soup cups, garnished with sliced cucumber.

Minestrone

Method

1 Prepare vegetables, toss carrot, leek, cabbage, celery and onion with melted butter, in a saucepan, do not brown.
2 Add the stock, seasoning and bouquet garni, bring to the boil and simmer for 20 minutes.
3 Add the other vegetables, spaghetti and tomato purée, cook for a further 10 minutes.
4 Mix the crushed garlic and chopped parsley together, add to soup just before serving.
5 Serve with grated parmesan cheese.

Ingredients

1 carrot, sliced
4 leeks, sliced
¼ cabbage, thinly sliced
1 stick celery, sliced
1 onion, sliced
50g (2oz) butter
1litre (2pt) stock
seasoning
bouquet garni
25g (1oz) peas
25g (1oz) french beans
100g (4oz) tomatoes
25g (1oz) spaghetti
1 5ml (tea) spoon tomato purée
1 clove garlic, crushed
parsley, chopped

French Onion Soup

Method

1 Fry the onion in the butter until soft and brown.
2 Add the stock and seasoning, bring to the boil, simmer for 45 minutes.   Pour into individual dishes.
3 Cut toast into small rounds or squares, place on the soup, sprinkle over the cheese and melt under the grill.

Ingredients

4 large onions, sliced
50g (2oz) butter
1litre (2pt) stock
seasoning
toast
cheese, grated

Mushroom Soup

Method

1 Slice mushrooms, keeping 6–8 sliced button mushrooms for garnishing (cook these in milk for a few minutes).
2 Fry onion in 25g (1oz) butter, do not brown, add the mushrooms, bouquet garni and stock, simmer for 25 minutes.
3 When tender, purée or pass through a sieve.
4 Melt remaining butter and make a roux with the flour and milk. Add the mushroom purée and bring to the boil, simmer for 5 minutes.
5 Add seasoning and garnish with sliced button mushrooms.

Ingredients

200g (8oz) button mushrooms
½ onion, chopped
50g (2oz) butter
bouquet garni
375ml (¾pt) stock
25g (1oz) flour
500ml (1pt) milk
seasoning

Tomato Soup

Method

1 Sauté the bacon and vegetables for 10 minutes.
2 Blend cornflour with a little stock, add to the rest of the stock. Add stock, bouquet garni and seasoning to the vegetables, bring to the boil, simmer for 1 hour.
3 Remove from the heat and purée or pass through a sieve, return to pan, add sugar, seasoning and cream. Adjust seasoning to taste. Serve with croutons.

Ingredients

100g (4oz) bacon, diced
1 stick celery, sliced
400g (1lb) tomatoes, quartered
1 carrot, chopped
25g (1oz) cornflour
750ml (1½pt) white stock
bouquet garni
freshly ground black pepper
pinch sugar
salt
1 15ml (table) spoon cream

Oxtail Soup

Method

1. Wash and drain the oxtail pieces and sauté in dripping with the prepared vegetables.
2. Cover with stock and bring to the boil adding bouquet garni, peppercorns and bacon.
3. Simmer for 2–3 hours, when meat is tender, skim fat off soup.
4. Strain and cut up the tender meat into small pieces.
5. Blend cornflour with cold water, add to soup with red wine and tomato purée.
6. Bring to the boil and cook gently, add meat pieces. Season and add more wine with a little lemon juice if necessary.

Ingredients

1 oxtail, cut into pieces
25g (1oz) dripping
1 stick celery, sliced
2 onions, chopped
1litre (2pt) stock
bouquet garni
6 peppercorns
50g (2oz) bacon, chopped
25g (1oz) cornflour
red wine
tomato purée
seasoning
lemon juice

Chicken Soup

Method

1. Simmer the chicken carcase, onion and peppercorns for 1½ hours in stock.
2. Strain and return liquor to the saucepan, add the cooked chicken and seasoning.
3. Blend the cornflour with a little cold water, add to the soup. Bring the soup to the boil and simmer for 5 minutes.
4. Add cream, sprinkle chopped parsley over the soup just before serving.

Ingredients

1 chicken carcase
1 large onion, sliced
6 peppercorns
750ml (1½pt) chicken stock
200g (8oz) cooked chicken, chopped
seasoning
1 15ml (table) spoon cornflour
1 15ml (table) spoon cream
parsley, chopped

Cold Soups

Vichyssoise

Method

1 Melt butter, add the leek and onion, fry gently for 5–10 minutes, do not brown.
2 Add the potatoes, stock and seasoning. Bring to the boil, skim off excess fat. Simmer for 30 minutes.
3 Sieve or purée, chill.
4 Add milk and cream. Worcester sauce may be added to give extra flavour.
5 Serve sprinkled with chives and parsley.

Ingredients

25g (1oz) butter
200g (8oz) leeks, sliced
1 onion, sliced
200g (8oz) potatoes, sliced
500ml (1pt) chicken stock
seasoning
125ml ($\frac{1}{4}$pt) milk
125ml ($\frac{1}{4}$pt) cream
worcester sauce
parsley
chives

Gazpacho

Method

1 Soak the breadcrumbs in the vinegar. Add the garlic.
2 Add half the cucumber, half the green pepper and all the onion, to the breadcrumbs and garlic.
3 Either blend or sieve. Add the oil slowly to the mixture.
4 Add tomatoes and iced water to make thin consistency.
5 Season and chill well. Add the remaining chopped cucumber and pepper. Serve.

Ingredients

40g (1$\frac{1}{2}$oz) breadcrumbs
2 15ml (table) spoon red wine vinegar
2 cloves garlic, pounded to a paste
with a pinch salt
1 cucumber, chopped
1 green pepper, chopped
1 onion, chopped
50ml (2fl oz) salad oil
1kg (2lb) tomatoes, sieved
iced water
seasoning

Sauces

A good sauce can be quite simple to make and will improve the flavour and appearance of many dishes. Sometimes the sauce forms the basis of a complete dish; pieces of cold meat may be added to a curry sauce and served with rice for a quick tasty meal, or a cheese sauce poured over cooked cauliflower, sprinkled with breadcrumbs and browned under the grill makes a delicious 'au gratin' dish. Jam sauce or chocolate sauce may be served with ice cream or steamed puddings. Cranberry and apple sauces are traditionally served with roast turkey and pork respectively.

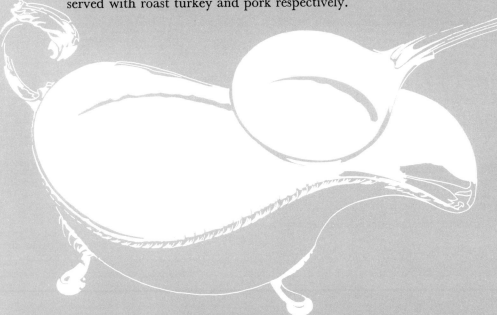

Basic White Sauce

Method

1 Melt the fat.
2 Remove from the heat and add the flour.
3 Return to heat, stir with wooden spoon until the roux resembles breadcrumbs.
4 Remove from the heat, add the milk gradually, beating all the time.
5 Return to the heat continue to beat until it comes to the boil and thickens.
6 Season.

Note: Part of the liquid quantity may be replaced by stock or wine.

Ingredients	Consistency
25g (1oz) flour 25g (1oz) margarine or butter 500ml (1pt) milk seasoning	pouring
25g (1oz) flour 25g (1oz) margarine or butter 250ml (½pt) milk seasoning	coating
25g (1oz) flour 25g (1oz) margarine or butter 125ml (¼pt) milk seasoning	panada

Variations of Basic White Sauces

These quantities are quoted for 250ml (½pt) basic sauce.

Anchovy   2 5ml (tea) spoon anchovy essence, few drops of lemon juice. Add to sauce just before serving.

Béchamel   Place with milk in a saucepan ½ carrot, ½ small onion, 1 piece celery, mace, clove and 6 white peppercorns. Bring to the boil, infuse for 10 mins, Strain. Use to make sauce.

Caper   1 15ml (table) spoon capers, 1 5ml (tea) spoon vinegar. Cook capers in sauce, add vinegar just before serving.

Cheese   50g (2oz) cheese, finely grated. Add before serving.

Egg   1 egg, hard boiled and finely chopped, add just before serving.

Mustard   1 5ml (tea) spoon made mustard, 2 5ml (tea) spoon vinegar. Cook mustard in sauce for 5 minutes, add vinegar just before serving.

Onion   200g (8oz) onions, boiled, drained and chopped well, add to sauce.

Parsley   2 5ml (tea) spoon parsley, chopped, cook in sauce for 5 minutes before serving.

Shrimp   50g (2oz) shrimps, peeled and a few drops anchovy essence. Cook for 5 minutes before serving.

Basic Brown Sauce

Method

1 Melt the fat, add carrot, turnip and onion. Fry until just golden brown.
2 Remove from heat and add the flour. Stir over a very low heat until the roux becomes a chestnut brown. A low heat is essential otherwise the mixture will burn and have a bitter taste.
3 Remove from heat, allow to cool before gradually adding the stock.
4 Bring to the boil, beating all the time, simmer for 10–15 minutes.
5 Season and strain; it may be necessary to skim off excess fat.

Ingredients

25g (1oz) dripping
carrot, sliced
turnip, sliced
onion, sliced
25g (1oz) flour
250ml (½pt) stock
seasoning

Espagnole Sauce

Method

1 Melt the fat, add bacon and vegetables. Fry gently until golden brown.
2 Remove from heat and add the flour. Stir over a very low heat until the roux becomes a chestnut brown.
3 Remove from heat, allow to cool before gradually adding the stock.
4 Bring to the boil, stirring all the time, simmer for 15 minutes.
5 Add the tomato purée and cook a further 15 minutes.
6 Season and strain, skim off fat if necessary.

Ingredients

25g (1oz) dripping
25g (1oz) lean ham or bacon, chopped
1 small onion, chopped
1 carrot, chopped
3–4 mushroom stalks
25g (1oz) flour
250ml (½pt) stock
bouquet garni
1 5ml (tea) spoon tomato purée
seasoning

Thick Gravy

Method

1 Pour off most of the fat from the roasting tin. Pour meat extract into a saucepan.
2 Sprinkle flour onto the meat extract.
3 Heat gently until the flour begins to brown.
4 Add stock, stirring all the time.
5 Simmer for 3–5 minutes.
6 Season and strain into heated gravy boat.

Ingredients

meat extract from roast joint
1–2 15ml (table) spoon plain flour
250–375ml ($\frac{1}{2}$–$\frac{3}{4}$pt) stock

Thin Gravy

Method

1 Pour off fat from roasting tin. Pour meat extract into a saucepan.
2 Add strained stock to meat extract.
3 Boil up, season to taste, strain into heated gravy boat.

Ingredients

meat extract from roast joint
250ml ($\frac{1}{2}$pt) stock

Tomato Sauce

Method

1 Place tomatoes, herbs, onion, water, meat extract, bacon and seasoning together in a saucepan. Bring to boil and simmer for 20–30 minutes.
2 Blend the cornflour with a little water and add to the saucepan.
3 Bring to the boil stirring continuously, cook for 3 minutes.
4 Sieve or blend, season and reheat.

Ingredients

300g (12oz) fresh or tinned tomatoes
pinch mixed herbs
1 onion, finely chopped
250ml ($\frac{1}{2}$pt) water
2 5ml (tea) spoon meat extract
1 rasher bacon, chopped
seasoning
2 5ml (tea) spoon cornflour

Curry Sauce

Method

1 Infuse the coconut in boiled stock for ½ hour, strain coconut and reserve stock.
2 Fry onion and apple in butter, add the curry powder, stir well.
3 Blend cornflour with some of the stock, add with the rest of the stock, lemon juice and salt to the fried ingredients.
4 Simmer for 2 hours in either the oven at 140–150°C or on the hob.
5 Add chutney and treacle before serving.

Ingredients

1 15ml (table) spoon dessicated coconut
250ml (½pt) stock
1 small onion, chopped
1 small apple, chopped
15g (½oz) butter
15–25g (½–1oz) curry powder
15g (½oz) cornflour
lemon juice
salt
1 15 ml (table) spoon chutney
1 15ml (table) spoon black treacle

Bread Sauce

Method

1 Stick cloves in onion, place in milk, bring to the boil.
2 Allow to infuse for 15 minutes, strain and add breadcrumbs to the milk. Reheat slowly adding butter and seasoning.
3 Just before serving, add cream.

Ingredients

3–4 cloves
1 onion
250ml (½pt) milk
75g (3oz) breadcrumbs
25g (1oz) butter
seasoning
1 15ml (table) spoon cream

Chocolate Sauce

Method

1 Break chocolate into pieces, place in saucepan with the sugar, cocoa and half the water, stir until boiling and the chocolate has dissolved.
2 Allow to simmer for 2 minutes then add the remaining water and vanilla essence. Boil for 15–20 minutes.

Ingredients

75g (3oz) dark chocolate
50g (2oz) sugar
1 5ml (tea) spoon cocoa
250ml (½pt) water
vanilla essence

c

Jam Sauce

Method

1 Blend arrowroot with a little of the water or fruit juice. Bring the remainder to the boil and pour over blended arrowroot.
2 Add jam and lemon juice.
3 Boil for 2 minutes, stirring all the time.

Ingredients

1 5ml (tea) spoon arrowroot
125ml ($\frac{1}{4}$pt) water or fruit juice
3 15ml (table) spoon jam
2 5ml (tea) spoon lemon juice

Cranberry Sauce

Method

1 Wash fruit, stew with water until soft, stirring occasionally.
2 Stir in sugar, allow to dissolve.
3 Add the port just before serving.

Ingredients

400g (1lb) fresh or frozen cranberries
65ml ($\frac{1}{8}$pt) water
200g (8oz) sugar
2 5ml (tea) spoon port

Egg Custard Sauce

Method

1 Whisk eggs and sugar together lightly.
2 Warm milk and lemon together, leave to infuse for 10 minutes.
3 Pour milk over eggs. Strain, place in a double saucepan.
4 Stir over a low heat until the sauce thickens and coats the back of a wooden spoon.

Ingredients

1$\frac{1}{2}$ eggs or 3 egg yolks
1 15ml (table) spoon sugar
250ml ($\frac{1}{2}$pt) milk
strip of lemon rind

Apple Sauce

Method

1 Prepare apples, cook over a gentle heat with other ingredients.
2 When cooked, beat well or sieve. Reheat and use as desired.

Ingredients

400g (1lb) cooking apples
15g ($\frac{1}{2}$oz) butter
sugar to taste
1 strip of lemon rind
water

Brandy Sauce

Method

1 Blend the cornflour with a little milk, boil the remainder and pour over blended cornflour.
2 Return to the pan, boil for 3–5 minutes stirring all the time.
3 Allow to cool, add the sugar, egg yolk and brandy.
4 Reheat, do not allow to boil. Serve at once.

Ingredients

2 5ml (tea) spoon cornflour
250ml ($\frac{1}{2}$pt) milk
40g (1$\frac{1}{2}$oz) sugar
1 egg yolk
3 15ml (table) spoon brandy

Arrowroot Glaze

Method

1 Blend arrowroot with little of the fruit juice. Bring the remainder to the boil and add to the blended arrowroot.
2 Add sugar, boil for a few minutes, stirring all the time, add colouring.

Ingredients

2 heaped 5ml (tea) spoon arrowroot
125ml ($\frac{1}{4}$pt) fruit juice
sugar to taste
colouring

Salad Dressings

Mayonnaise

Method

1 Ensure that all ingredients are at room temperature.
2 Mix egg yolks, sugar and mustard in a mixing bowl.
3 Slowly add a thin stream of salad oil to the mixture, beating all the time. Season.
4 Add enough lemon juice to thin mixture down to correct consistency.

Note: If using a blender one whole egg can be used. Place all ingredients except the oil into the blender. Switch on to maximum speed and pour in the oil slowly. Season and serve.

Ingredients

2 egg yolks
½ 5ml (tea) spoon sugar
½ 5ml (tea) spoon mustard
125ml (¼pt) salad oil
seasoning
15ml (table) spoon lemon juice

Variations

For tartare sauce add:
1 5ml (tea) spoon gherkins, chopped
1 5ml (tea) spoon capers, chopped
½ 5ml (tea) spoon parsley, chopped
½ 5ml (tea) spoon tarragon, chopped
(optional)

French Dressing

Method

1 Mix the seasoning with the oil.
2 Place with the vinegar in a tightly lidded bottle or screw top jar. Shake until thick and well emulsified.

Note: If using a blender, place all ingredients in blender, turn to maximum speed for a few seconds.

Ingredients

½ 5ml (tea) spoon ground pepper
½ 5ml (tea) spoon salt
pinch dry mustard
3 15ml (table) spoon salad oil
1 15ml (table) spoon wine vinegar

Fish Cookery

Fish is a good source of protein and can be served at any meal time. Kedgeree, traditionally served as a breakfast dish, is now more likely to form part of a lunch or supper meal. In this section there are recipes given for the more usual methods of cooking fish as well as fish dishes which may be served as starters, fish courses and main courses.

Preparation

Flat fish   Remove head and entrails. Wash fish well, using salt to clean away dark skin.

Round fish   Remove head, make a slit on the underside towards the tail, remove entrails. Wash fish well, using salt to clean away dark skin.

Other preparation   Remove fins and loose scales. Replace roe if desired. Dry.

Methods of Cooking Fish

Baked fish   Place prepared fish on a baking tray or in an ovenware dish. Sprinkle with seasoning and lemon juice. Dot with butter or margarine. Cover with greased paper.

Thin pieces of fish, e.g. fillets, may be placed on greaseproof paper for easy removal. Fold, roll or place fish in layers to keep moist during cooking.

Allow 10-30 minutes, depending on thickness of fish. To test, insert a knife in a thick part, which should look creamy white when cooked. Cook in a moderate oven.

Serve with sauce, e.g. parsley, anchovy, etc.

Baked stuffed fish   Prepare fish, spread and roll or fill the cavity with parsley & thyme stuffing (page 71). Cover and cook in a moderate oven.

Steamed fish   Steaming is suitable for fillets and fish steaks. Prepare fish, season and sprinkle with lemon juice. Steam on a plate over boiling water. To test, insert a knife in a thick part, which should look creamy white when cooked. Serve with sauce, e.g. parsley, anchovy, etc.

Grilled Fish

Grilling is suitable for herrings, mackerel, kippers, flat fish and fish steaks. Prepare fish, score the skin to allow the heat to penetrate, grill. Oily fish such as herrings do not need to be brushed with oil, but white fish, such as sole and plaice, require to be brushed liberally with melted fat or oil before and during grilling. To test, insert a knife in a thick part, which should look creamy white when cooked.

Deep fried Fish

Deep frying is suitable for fillets, small steaks and small whole fish. Shallow frying is suitable for thicker pieces of fish and all oily fish. Prepare fish, season and coat with seasoned flour, egg and breadcrumbs or coating batter (page 73). Fill a deep pan one third full of fat or oil. Heat to 180°C (360°F). Using a wire basket, lower in the fish and cook for 5–10 minutes depending on thickness. Drain on kitchen paper.

Poached Fish

Poaching is suitable for fillets, fish steaks and small whole fish. Prepare fish, place in a saucepan containing a small amount of boiling milk or water. To test, insert a knife in a thick part, which should look creamy white when cooked. Remove carefully. Serve with sauce, e.g. cheese, caper.

Plaice in Mushroom Sauce

Method

1 Wash and dry the fillets, sprinkle with lemon juice and seasoning, and roll from head to tail, place in greased casserole dish.
2 Combine the soup, milk or white wine and a 5ml (tea) spoon of lemon juice.
3 Pour over the plaice, cover with buttered greaseproof paper and bake.

Ingredients

4 large fillets plaice
(approx 1kg (2lb))
juice of $\frac{1}{2}$ lemon
seasoning
1 tin condensed cream of mushroom soup
1 15ml (table) spoon milk (or white wine)

Cooking

Main oven temperature:
180–190°C
Time: 25–35 mins
Dish: ovenware dish
Shelf: middle

Second oven
temperature: 170–180°C
Fan oven
temperature: 170°C

Serves 4

Fish Pie

Method

1 Peel the potatoes, cook them in boiling salted water until tender. Drain and sieve the potatoes and cream them with the knob of butter and 2 15ml (table) spoon milk.
2 Poach the fish in the milk until just cooked. Drain the fish, reserving the milk. Remove the skin and any bones from the fish and flake.
3 Make a white sauce with the flour, butter or margarine and the reserved milk. Add the seasoning, parsley, and lemon juice and mix well together.
4 Stir in the fish and place in an oven casserole dish.
5 Pipe the potato over the top of the fish and bake in a hot oven until the potato is brown.

Variations

The parsley sauce can be replaced by a white sauce to which one of the following may be added.

Ingredients

$\frac{1}{2}$–$\frac{3}{4}$kg (1–1$\frac{1}{2}$lb) potatoes
knob of butter
2 15ml (table) spoon milk
400g (1lb) cod or haddock
250ml ($\frac{1}{2}$pt) milk
25g (1oz) flour
25g (1oz) butter or margarine
seasoning
1 15ml (table) spoon parsley, chopped
a little lemon juice

Variations

100g (4oz) mushrooms, chopped
100g (4oz) prawns, peeled
50–75g (2–3oz) cheese, grated

Cooking

Main oven temperature: 210°C
Time: 20–25 mins
Dish: ovenware dish
Shelf: top/middle

Second oven
temperature: 190–200°C
Fan oven
temperature: 190°C

Serves 4–6

Russian Fish Pie

Method

1 Make up pastry and white sauce.
2 Remove skin and bones from fish. Mix the fish, white sauce, parsley, lemon juice and seasoning together.
3 Roll out pastry into a square 30 × 30cm (12 × 12in.) trim edges. Place on a baking tray. Place the filling in the centre. Damp edges, fold each corner into the centre, forming an envelope. Seal edges, brush with beaten egg.
4 Cut leaves from remaining pastry, place along joins, brush leaves with beaten egg. Carefully lift leaf and make small incisions at each join, this will allow steam to escape and pastry will be more crisp and light. Bake.

Ingredients

200g (8oz) flaky pastry (page 128)
125ml (¼pt) white sauce (panada) (page 30)
300g (12oz) cooked fish
2 5ml (tea) spoon parsley, chopped
2 5ml (tea) spoon lemon juice
seasoning
egg, beaten

Cooking

Main oven temperature: 230°C
Time: 30–40 mins
Tin: baking tray
Shelf: top/middle
Second oven temperature: 210–220°C
Fan oven temperature: 210°C

Serves 4–6

Kedgeree

Method

1 Boil the rice in the normal way (page 67.)
2 Wash and trim the fish, place in a saucepan and just cover the fish with cold water.
3 Bring the fish to the boil slowly. Turn off the hotplate and leave to stand for 10 minutes. Drain and flake the fish, discarding the skin and bones.
4 Chop one hard boiled egg and slice the other.
5 Melt the butter in a large saucepan, lightly fry the onion until cooked but not browned.
6 Add the rice, fish and chopped hard boiled egg and seasoning. Mix well together and leave to warm through for 5–10 minutes.
7 Serve in a heated dish and garnish with sliced hard boiled eggs and chopped parsley.

Ingredients

150g (6oz) patna rice
300g (12oz) smoked haddock
2 eggs, hard boiled
50g (2oz) butter
1 small onion, chopped
seasoning
parsley, chopped

Serves 4

Trout and Almonds

Method

1. Clean the fish but leave the heads on. Wash and wipe them and dip into the seasoned flour.
2. Melt 100g (4oz) butter and fry 2 of the fish until they are tender and golden, turning them once. Remove the fish and cook the remaining 2.
3. Clean the pan and melt the rest of the butter. Add the almonds and cook until lightly browned.
4. Add a squeeze of lemon juice and pour over the fish.
5. Serve at once with wedges of lemon.

Ingredients

4 trout (about 100–125g (4–5oz) each)
seasoned flour
150g (6oz) butter or margarine
50–75g (2–3oz) almonds, blanched and cut into slivers
juice ½ lemon
lemon wedges

Serves 4

Soused Herrings–Roll Mops

Method

1. Clean and bone the herrings. Roll up tightly from the tail end.
2. Place in a pie dish with the onion, herbs and seasoning, cover with the vinegar and water.
3. Bake in a moderate oven. Allow to cool in the cooking liquor.

Ingredients

4 fresh herrings
¼ 5ml (tea) spoon salt
1 piece mace
1 bay leaf
6 peppercorns
2 cloves
125ml (¼pt) vinegar
125ml (¼pt) water
1 onion, chopped (optional)

Cooking

Main oven temperature: 180°C
Time: 25–35 mins
Dish: ovenware dish
Shelf: middle
Second oven temperature: 170–180°C
Fan oven temperature: 170°C

Serves 4

Mackerel in Oatmeal

Method

1. Clean the fish, remove the bones, head and tail and then wash in cold water.
2. Sprinkle with seasoning and then dip the fish in the oatmeal or rolled oats, pressing the oats well onto the fish.
3. Gently fry the fish in the butter or margarine. Serve sprinkled with chopped parsley and wedges of lemon.

Ingredients

4 mackerel
seasoning
fine oatmeal or rolled oats
100g (4oz) butter or margarine for frying

Note: Herrings in oatmeal can be prepared and cooked in the same way.

Serves 4

Poached Haddock with Eggs

Method

1 Poach haddock gently in milk and water.
2 When cooked, drain well and place on a hot dish.
3 Keep warm, whilst poaching the eggs in the fish liquor.
4 Place a poached egg on the haddock and dot with small knobs of butter, Serve immediately.

Ingredients

medium size smoked haddock
(per person)
125ml ($\frac{1}{4}$pt) water
125ml ($\frac{1}{4}$pt) milk
1 egg (per person)
butter

Haddock with Bacon

Method

1 Wipe the fillets and place on a greased grid. Brush well with melted butter and seasoning.
2 Place under a hot grill and cook for 5 minutes.
3 Lay the slices of streaky bacon over the fish and continue grilling until the bacon is cooked.

Ingredients

4 golden haddock fillets
50g (2oz) butter, melted
seasoning
4 rashers streaky bacon

Serves 4

Fish Cakes

Method

1 Mash fish, remove bones. Mash potatoes. Mix together with egg, lemon, seasoning, and parsley.
2 Place on a floured board and divide into 6. Shape each portion into a flat round circle.
3 Coat with flour, egg, and breadcrumbs. Fry in hot fat or grill until heated through. Serve with parsley sauce.

Ingredients

200g (8oz) cooked fish
100g (4oz) cooked potatoes
$\frac{1}{2}$ egg
juice and rind of $\frac{1}{2}$ lemon, finely grated
seasoning
$\frac{1}{2}$ 5ml (tea) spoon parsley, chopped
seasoned flour
egg, beaten
breadcrumbs

Makes 6

43

Shell Fish

Dressed Crab

Method

1 Pull the shell apart from the body (to which the claws are attached).
2 Take the shell and remove the stomach bag (which is found just below the head). Discard this.
3 Carefully scrape all the meat from the shell into a basin, this is called the soft or dark meat.
4 Wash and if necessary, scrub the shell, dry and rub with a little oil to give a shine.
5 Knock away the edge of the shell as far as the dark line around the rim.
6 Add breadcrumbs to the brown meat, season with salt, pepper, lemon juice and add a little chopped parsley. Pack this mixture into the sides of the shell, leaving a space in the middle for the white meat.
7 Take the body section, remove and discard the 'dead man's' fingers (greyish white pieces) which are inedible.
8 Crack the claws (except the very small ones) with a weight and take out all the white meat from the claws and body. Use a skewer to reach the crevices, and be careful not to get any splinters of the shell with the meat!
9 Season the flesh with salt, pepper, cayenne and vinegar, and pile into the centre of the shell.
10 Decorate the crab with a little paprika and chopped parsley and serve on a bed of lettuce. Garnish with the small claws.

Ingredients

1 cooked crab
1–2 15ml (table) spoon fresh breadcrumbs
seasoning
lemon juice
parsley, chopped
cayenne pepper
vinegar
paprika pepper

Serves 2–4

Scampi Provençale

Method

1 Fry the onion and garlic gently in the butter or margarine until cooked but not browned.
2 Add tomatoes, wine, seasoning, sugar and parsley, stir well and simmer gently for 10 minutes.
3 Drain the scampi well, add to the sauce and continue simmering for about 5 minutes, or until they are just heated through.
4 Serve with crusty french bread, or boiled rice.

Ingredients

1 onion, chopped
1 clove of garlic, chopped
25g (1oz) butter or margarine
1 375g (15oz) tin tomatoes, drained
4 15ml (table) spoon dry white wine
seasoning
pinch sugar
1 15ml (table) spoon parsley, chopped
200g (8oz) frozen scampi, thawed

Serves 4

Lobster Thermidor

Method

1 Remove the lobster meat from the shells discarding the stomach, intestine and spongy looking gills. Chop the claw and head meat and cut the meat from the tail into thick slices.
2 Melt 25g (1oz) butter in a saucepan and add the onion, parsley and tarragon. After a few minutes add the wine and simmer for 5 minutes.
3 Add the béchamel sauce and simmer until reduced to a creamy consistency.
4 Add the lobster meat, seasoning, remaining butter and 2 15ml (table) spoon of the cheese.
5 Arrange the mixture in the shells. Sprinkle with the remaining cheese and put under the grill to brown the top quickly. Serve at once.

Ingredients

2 small or 1 large cooked lobster
50g (2oz) butter
1 15ml (table) spoon onion, chopped
2 15ml (table) spoon parsley, chopped
1–2 15ml (table) spoon tarragon, chopped
4 15ml (table) spoon white wine
250ml ($\frac{1}{2}$pt) béchamel sauce (page 30)
pinch mustard, salt, paprika pepper
3 15ml (table) spoon parmesan cheese, grated

Serves 4

Scampi in Batter

Method

1 Frozen scampi should be thawed and dried before use.
2 Make a well in the flour, add the oil and half the water.
3 Beat well and gradually add the remaining water. Whisk the egg white and add the flour mixture and mix well together.
4 Meanwhile, heat the deep fat for frying.
5 Add the scampi to the batter and when the oil is hot, drop 5ml (tea) spoons of scampi and batter into the hot oil and fry until golden brown. (3–4 minutes)
6 Drain the scampi on kitchen paper.
7 Serve the scampi in a warm dish and hand tartare sauce separately, (page 36).

Ingredients

75–100g (3–4oz) Dublin bay prawns (scampi), prepared weight
50g (2oz) plain flour ⎫ sieved
pinch salt ⎭ together
1 10ml (dessert) spoon oil
65ml (⅛ pt) water
1 egg white
deep fat for frying

Serves 2–3

Scallops Gratinées

Method

1 If the scallops are in the shells, remove them, wash and keep the shells. Rinse scallops in cold water and place in a saucepan. Add water and wine, bring to the boil and cook for 10 minutes.
2 Meanwhile fry onion and mushrooms in oil until soft.
3 Drain off excess oil and mix parsley, seasoning with the mushrooms and onion.
4 Place a spoonful of this mixture into the 4 shells or individual dishes.
5 Place two drained scallops in each dish and cover with the remaining mushroom mixture.
6 Sprinkle with breadcrumbs and dot with butter.
7 Place under a hot grill to crisp the crumbs.

Ingredients

8 scallops
125ml (¼pt) water
125ml (¼pt) white wine
1 small onion, chopped
200g (8oz) mushrooms, chopped
2 15ml (table) spoon oil
1 15ml (table) spoon parsley, chopped
seasoning
fresh breadcrumbs
butter

Serves 4

Meat Cookery

Meat provides the main source of protein in the diet of most families and whether you prefer your meat roasted, grilled, fried or casseroled, this section includes cooking methods and recipes to interest most tastes. When buying meat, if in doubt, be guided by your butcher as he is the best judge of the meat he has in stock. After choosing carefully, expert preparation and cooking is the key to ensure that the dish is the centre of attraction at any meal table.

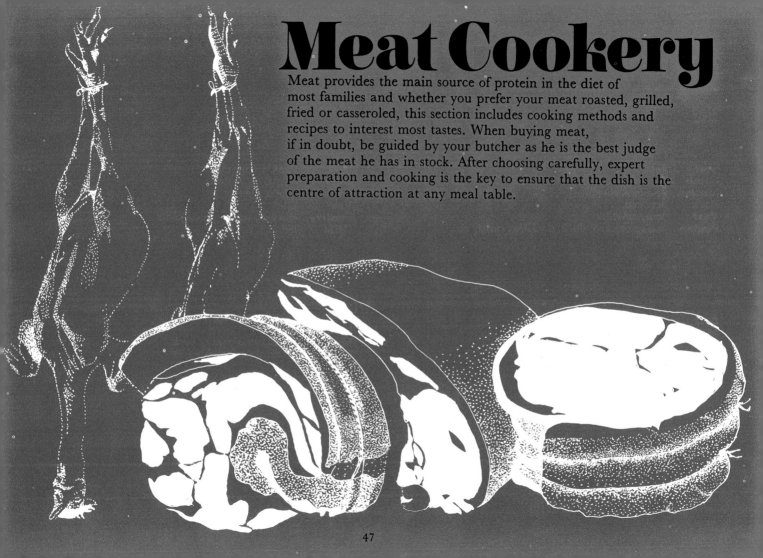

47

Choice of Meat and Poultry

Certain joints are more suitable for one cooking method than another, below is a list to guide you:

Roasting

Beef topside, sirloin, ribs
Lamb leg, loin, best end of neck, shoulder, breast (stuffed)
Mutton leg, loin, shoulder
Pork leg, loin
Veal loin, shoulder
Poultry spring chicken, duck, duckling, turkey etc.

Grilling

Beef steak, rump, fillet
Lamb chops, leg cutlets
Pork chops, fillet
Veal fillet
Poultry chicken, turkey, duck joints
Offal kidneys, liver

Boiling

Beef silverside, brisket, shin
Mutton leg
Pork ham, bacon, belly
Poultry boiling fowl
Offal kidneys, tongue, brains, sweetbreads

Stewing

Beef brisket, shin, tail
Lamb breast
Mutton breast, scrag end of neck
Veal breast, knuckle, shoulder

Methods of Cooking Meat and Poultry

The times given below will be a guide when cooking meat, but slight adjustments may be necessary.

1 Size of joint: A small one takes longer per pound than a large one. (Up to 30 minutes longer for a small joint weighing 1kg (2lb only).
2 A short, thick joint takes longer than a thinner one.
3 Boned and rolled joints take longer to cook through than those with the bone left in.
4 Personal preference e.g. rare, medium, well done.
5 Meat with a thick layer of fat takes longer than a lean joint
6 Poultry should be thawed completely before cooking.

Due to the low temperature at which frozen meat is stored, it could take a considerable time to thaw out and regain room temperature.

Alternative ways of thawing a 1½–2kg (3–4lb) piece topside beef:

1 Remove meat from freezer and place in a refrigerator approximately 72hrs before it is needed.
2 Remove meat from freezer and place in a refrigerator approximately 48hrs before it is needed; take out of the refrigerator overnight.
3 Remove from freezer and thaw at room temperature for 24hrs. Smaller, flatter joints, such as shoulder of lamb or loin of pork will take less time. If a joint is still chilled in the centre when it is required for cooking, allow slightly longer cooking. DO NOT COOK POULTRY UNTIL IT IS COMPLETELY THAWED THROUGHOUT.

Aluminium Foil

When foil is used the cooking time should be increased. To brown and crisp the exterior of the joint remove the foil for the last 20–30 minutes of the cooking period.

Preparation for Roasting

Wipe meat, place in roasting tin (on trivet if supplied), fat side uppermost. Brush with melted fat, the amount depends on type of meat, e.g. veal requires more than pork. Lean joints, e.g. veal, also poultry and game may be covered with strips of fat or basted in the usual way.

Stewing

Stewing is suitable for the cheaper, coarser cuts of meat.
Remove fat and cut meat into small even sized pieces, or leave
whole as desired.
Flavouring ingredients are usually added, e.g. onion, carrot,
turnip, mixed herbs, seasoning. Add liquid. Cover with a tight
fitting lid, cook slowly until meat is tender. Never let a stew boil.

Grilling

Choose meat as for frying.
Wipe meat and remove surplus fat. Grill.
Meat to be grilled may also be steeped in marinade before
cooking. This will produce more tender results.

Boiling

Wipe meat. Trim remove bone if necessary, tie into compact
shape. Place meat in boiling water, allow to boil for 5 minutes.
Reduce heat and simmer for required time.

Fresh meat	20 minutes per $\frac{1}{2}$kg (1 lb) + 20 minutes
Salt meat	25 minutes per $\frac{1}{2}$kg (1 lb) + 25 minutes
Bacon, tongue	30 minutes per $\frac{1}{2}$kg (1 lb) + 30 minutes
Poultry $1\frac{1}{2}$–2kg (3–4 lb)	1–$2\frac{1}{2}$ hours according to age.

Frying

The more expensive cuts of meat are cooked by this method.
Wipe meat, remove surplus fat. Brown each side of the meat at
a fairly high temperature, reduce heat and continue cooking at
a lower temperature until tender.

Roasting Chart

Meat	Conventional main oven temp.	Second/fan oven temp.	Cooking time
Beef	190–200°C	180–190°C	20–35 minutes per ½kg (1lb) and 20–35 minutes over
Beef, boned	190–200°C	180–190°C	25–35 minutes per ½kg (1lb) and 25–35 minutes over
Mutton and lamb	190–200°C	180–190°C	25–35 minutes per ½kg (1lb) and 25–35 minutes over
Pork and veal	190–200°C	180–190°C	30–40 minutes per ½kg (1lb) and 30–40 minutes over
Ham	190–200°C	180–190°C	30–40 minutes per ½kg (1lb) and 30–40 minutes over
Chicken	190–200°C	180–190°C	15–20 minutes per ½kg (1lb) and 20 minutes over
Turkey and goose	190–200°C	180–190°C	15–20 minutes per ½kg (1lb) up to 3½kg (7lb) then 10 minutes per ½kg (1lb)
Duck	190–200°C	180–190°C	25–35 minutes per ½kg (1lb) and 25–30 minutes over
Pheasant	190–200°C	180–190°C	35–40 minutes per ½kg (1lb) and 35–40 minutes over
Potatoes with meat	190–200°C	180–190°C	according to size
Potatoes without meat	200–220°C	190–200°C	according to size

Grilling and Grilling Times

Bacon

Remove rind from bacon and make a few cuts in the fat side to prevent curling.

Bacon and eggs

Heat fat in grill pan until hot and drop in the eggs one by one. Cook under the grill for one minute and then place the grill grid or trivet with bacon on it over the top. Prepare the bacon as above. As the bacon cooks, the fat will fall on to the eggs giving them a delightful flavour.

Chicken portions

Wipe chicken portions and dry well. Brush with melted butter or oil and sprinkle with salt and pepper.

Steak

The more tender cuts of meat should be chosen for grilling. Brush the steaks and the grill pan, grid or trivet with melted butter or oil. Season the steaks well. Preheat the grill then place the steaks under it sealing both sides of the steaks well. The time allowed for grilling depends entirely on the cut and thickness of the steaks and personal preference.

Steaks average thickness	Rare	3–6 minutes each side
	Medium	6–8 minutes each side
	Well done	7–10 minutes each side
Pork chops		10–13 minutes each side
Chicken joints		10–15 minutes each side
Bacon rashers		2–3 minutes each side
Gammon rashers		5–8 minutes each side
Lamb chops		7–10 minutes each side
Lambs liver		5–10 minutes each side
Lambs kidneys		4–6 minutes each side
Sausages		10–20 minutes, turning as required

Roasting on the Spit

Preparation of Joints

All meat should be wiped with a damp cloth and trimmed of any surplus fat or gristle, etc. It should then be placed on the spit as explained below.

LAMB AND MUTTON

Legs with bone

Insert spit along the side of the bone in approximate centre of the joint.

Legs boned and rolled

Insert spit lengthwise through the centre.

Shoulder

This must be boned and can be filled with stuffing before being rolled and trussed. Again insert spit lengthwise through the centre of the joint.

Loin

Tie down the thin (rib) ends and place spit at right angles to bones through the thick part of the meat as near the centre as possible, or your butcher will 'chine' and truss it to make it more compact. Again insert spit lengthwise through the centre of the joint.

VEAL

Can be treated as lamb, above, and provided the joint is free to rotate and is centred on the spit, the meat will cook perfectly—fillets, rolled and trussed are particularly good, especially when filled with veal stuffing.

BEEF

Sirloin

Ask your butcher to chine it, being careful to remove the backbone; when trussed it will be very easy to insert the spit lengthwise.

Wing ribs, topside, aitchbone, fore and middle ribs

Can also be cooked to perfection on your spit—bone and truss to a convenient shape.

PORK

Leg

Prepare generally as for lamb or mutton. Full leg is too big to be accommodated on the spit. The knuckle end can be treated as for leg of lamb, but the fillet should be turned at right angles so that the spit is again lengthwise through the joint.

Loin

As for loin of lamb—but there is no need to truss as the ribs are cut off much shorter.

Whole fillet

Insert spit lengthwise through the centre of the joint.

CHICKEN

All poultry and game must be well trussed.
Two chickens or three poussins may be roasted by nesting together, their tail ends in the centre of the spit rod. Alternatively, one much larger chicken may also be spit roasted. When cooking has commenced brush once or twice with oil. This gives a very attractive dark golden colour to the skin.

GOOSE AND DUCK

To cook either—prepare with normal stuffing as for oven roasting and prick the skin all over with a fork and then position them lengthwise on your spit.

TURKEY

After stuffing and trussing, the spit should be inserted as centrally as possible through the bird.

GAME

See Roasting Chart on page 51
for cooking times and oven temperatures When the grill is used on some models for roasting on the spit, refer to your instruction booklet for the settings required.

Pheasants, grouse and partridge may all be cooked as for chicken and duck above—the smaller the bird, the more may be cooked 'in tandem' nested into one another as for chicken.
Fat bacon may be trussed onto the game and then the basting will be automatic. Otherwise, occasionally baste with melted bacon fat during the cooking.

Kebab Cookery

The general rules for kebab cookery are:

1 Choose even size pieces.
2 Leave a small space between each piece of food to allow heat to penetrate all sides.
3 Marinade or brush with oil to prevent drying.
4 Parboil foods which take a long time to cook through, e.g. small onions, potatoes.
5 Place food firmly on the kebab skewer. Mushrooms and peppers will not break if blanched first.
6 Food lacking in fat should be blended with fatty foods, e.g. liver and bacon, kidney and bacon.
7 Choose foods which require the same cooking time. (See list of ingredients.)

Suitable Foods for Kebab Cookery

2.5–4cm (1–1½in.) squares—lean prime quality lamb, pork, beef and veal; kidney; bacon slices and cubes; small sausages, tomatoes and mushrooms; small parboiled potatoes and onions.

The following foods need heating and browning only, and the cooking time should be adjusted as necessary.

Ham, liver sausage, luncheon meat, spam, salami cubes or slices, rolled into convenient pieces; frankfurters, prawns, cocktail onions, peppers (blanch first), cucumber, gherkins, olives, tinned carrots, cooked beetroot, pineapple, cherries (glacé or marachino), orange slices, apple quarters, dates.

SERVING

When serving, do not try to push more than 2 or 3 cubes off the kebab fork at one time, or you may squash the softer pieces.

Marinades

Here is your chance to give a new taste to cooking using a wide assortment of food. Meat, poultry, fish, vegetables, fruit, can all be cooked on kebab skewers.
Enhance the flavour by brushing with oil or sauce, or steeping in a piquant mixture of oil and flavouring.

Allow extra time to steep food in a marinade before cooking, this will produce very good results. Marinades are simply pickling media made with vinegar, oil, tomato or lemon juice, flavouring and seasoning.

The recipe of a typical marinade is given on page 57 but the ingredients may be varied with the exception of oil, which is included to prevent charring. Having made the marinade, steep the meat, for a few hours.

Allow meat to regain room temperature if refrigerated during the steeping time.

Cooking

The kebabs may be cooked on your kebab attachment if supplied, at 190°C–200°C for 40–60 minutes, depending on the type of food to be cooked, or on skewers under the grill, turning as necessary.

Roast Turkey

Make up the parsley and thyme stuffing (page 71) increasing the quantity according to the size of the bird (i.e. for 7½kg (16lb) turkey allow 400g (1lb) breadcrumbs, 200g (8oz) suet). Place the stuffing in the neck end of the bird, sausage meat can be placed in the cavity. Truss securely and season well. Heat a little dripping and brush over the breast of the bird, the breast can be covered with strips of streaky bacon. Place in the roasting tin (on trivet if supplied) and cover the bird with greased greaseproof paper or foil.

Cooking Ham or Gammon

Method

Soak the ham or gammon for 24 hours preferably, or at least overnight, changing the water occasionally. Dry well. Weigh after soaking as the cooking times are calculated on the soaked weight.

Cooking

Boiled: Place the ham or gammon in a pan of fresh cold water and bring slowly to the boil, reduce heat and simmer for the required cooking time. 20 minutes to the ½kg (1lb) and 20 minutes extra.
When cooked remove the joint from the liquid. Carefully remove the rind and sprinkle the fat with freshly toasted breadcrumbs.

Baked: Brush with melted fat and wrap in aluminium foil. Bake in a preheated oven for the amount of time shown on roasting chart. Thirty minutes from the end of cooking time, remove the foil to allow the steam to escape. Remove the rind.
1 Either gash the fat in several places and stick cloves into the fat and spread with glaze mixture.
2 Or spread with glaze mixture and decorate with slices of pineapple and glace cherries.
Turn the oven up 30°C and return the ham to the oven for 15–30 minutes to allow the sugar to caramelise. Serve hot or allow to cool and then slice thinly.

Glaze

25g (1oz) brown sugar
25g (1oz) butter
1 5ml (tea) spoon dried mustard
seasoning
} mix together.

Mixed Grill

Method

Prepare the ingredients as follows:

Lamb cutlets:	Wipe and then brush with melted lard or oil. Season well.
Sausages:	Prick with a fork in several places.
Bacon rolls:	Remove the rind from the slices of streaky bacon and smooth on a board with a palette knife until the slices are very thin. Cut the kidneys and the bananas in half and roll up tightly in the bacon.
Liver:	Dip the washed and dried liver slices in seasoned flour.
Mushrooms:	Brush with melted butter or oil and season.
Tomatoes:	Cut in half and make a cut in the top of each half. Place a little butter on this and season well.

Preheat the grill and well grease the grill pan, grid or trivet. Place tomatoes and mushrooms under the grid or trivet and other ingredients on the grid or trivet, allowing grilling times as given in the grilling chart. Serve garnished with watercress.

Ingredients

4 lamb cutlets
4 sausages
8 slices streaky bacon
4 kidneys
2 bananas
4 slices liver
200g (8oz) mushrooms
4 tomatoes
watercress

Serves 4

Marinades

Method

Mix all ingredients together and shake well. To do this place in a small screw-top jar and shake or place in a blender and turn to maximum speed for a few seconds.

Other Ingredients for Marinades

Herbs and spices: chilli powder, black pepper, cloves, rosemary, thyme, cinnamon, bayleaf, ginger, sage. *Sauces:* ketchup, worcester, tabasco, soy. *Vineger:* cider, wine, tarragon. *Various indgreients:* brown sugar, fruit juices, garlic, onion, salt, mustard, tomato puree, horse-radish.

Ingredients

125ml ($\frac{1}{4}$pt) pineapple juice
2 15ml (table) spoon soy sauce
$\frac{1}{2}$ clove garlic, finely chopped
65ml ($\frac{1}{8}$pt) salad oil
3 15ml (tea) spoon made mustard
1$\frac{1}{2}$ 15ml (table) spoon worcester sauce
1 15ml (table) spoon brown sugar
a few drops tabasco
1$\frac{1}{2}$ 15ml (table) spoon vinegar
salt
3 15ml (table) spoon tomato ketchup

Steak and Mushroom Pie

Method

1 Toss steak and kidney in seasoned flour.
2 Melt lard, fry onion, then add meat and mushrooms, pour off excess fat, add water and stock cubes, bring to the boil and then simmer until the meat is cooked.
3 Allow to cool and place in pie dish with pie funnel.
4 Roll out the pastry a little larger than dish, cut off a strip about 12mm ($\frac{1}{2}$in.) wide. Damp and press this strip of pastry onto the edge of the dish. Cover with the rolled out pastry. Trim and decorate edges, make a hole in pastry at top of pie funnel to allow steam to escape.
See illustration opposite page 128.

Ingredients

600g (1$\frac{1}{2}$lb) braising steak, cut into small pieces
6 lambs kidneys, cut into small pieces
1 15ml (table) spoon seasoned flour
25g (1oz) lard
1 onion, chopped
75g (3oz) mushrooms, sliced
125ml ($\frac{1}{4}$pt) water
1-2 stock cubes
400g (1lb) flaky pastry (page 128)

Cooking

Main oven temperature: 230°C
Time: 30–40 mins
Dish: ovenware dish
Shelf: top/middle
[Second oven temperature: 210–220°C
Fan oven temperature: 210°C]

Serves 4–6

Sausage Toad

Method

1 Place lard in tin and heat in oven.
2 Mix herbs with batter, pour in tin.
3 Arrange sausages in mixture, bake until golden brown and well risen.

Ingredients

25g (1oz) lard
2 5ml (tea) spoon mixed herbs
250ml ($\frac{1}{2}$pt) pouring batter (page 74)
300g (12oz) sausages, remove skins

Cooking

Main oven temperature: 220°C
Time: 45–60 mins
Tin: 18 × 28 × 2·5cm
(7 × 11 × 1in.)
Shelf: top
[Second oven temperature: 190–200°C
Fan oven temperature: 200–210°C]

Serves 4

Stuffed Hearts

Method

1 Soak hearts in cold salt water for 30 minutes, clean thoroughly. Remove pipes and trim. Stuff with sage and onion stuffing, (page 72). Secure tops with thread.
2 Melt butter and fry onions, remove and fry the hearts until brown.
3 Blend cornflour with a little of the stock and add to the remainder.
4 Place the onions and hearts in base of dish. Add thickened stock and seasoning. Cover with foil.

Ingredients

4 sheep's hearts
sage and onion stuffing (page 72)
25g (1oz) butter
2 onions, sliced
1 15ml (table) spoon cornflour
250ml (½pt) stock
seasoning

Cooking

Main oven temperature: 150°C
Time: 2–2½ hrs
Dish: ovenware dish
Shelf: middle
Second oven temperature: 140–150°C
Fan oven temperature: 130–140°C

Serves 4

Steak and Kidney Pudding

Method

1 Wash kidneys, soak in cold salt water for 5 minutes. Cut into small pieces.
2 Toss steak in seasoned flour.
3 Roll out two thirds of the pastry and line the basin. Add meat and onions in layers. Add stock, enough to cover half the meat.
4 Cover with remaining pastry, press moistened edges together to seal.
5 Cover with aluminium foil, greased greaseproof paper or cloth. Secure.
6 Steam in a steamer over a saucepan of boiling water or:
7 Place in a saucepan of boiling water with a tight fitting lid. Water should come halfway up the basin. When adding water to maintain level, it must be boiling.

Ingredients

200g (8oz) kidney
400g (1lb) steak, cut into cubes
3 15ml (table) spoon flour
seasoning
2 onions, sliced
125ml (¼pt) stock
300g (12oz) suet pastry (page 126)

Cooking

Time 3–4 hrs
Dish: ¾–1 litre (1½–2pt) pudding basin

Serves 4–6

Shepherds Pie

Method

1 Cook onion in stock until tender, add worcester sauce, nutmeg, breadcrumbs, seasoning and meat. Mix thoroughly and place in greased dish.
2 Mash potato, add butter and egg. Beat well and place on top of meat; smooth over and bake.

Note: Fresh meat may be used in this recipe. Proceed as follows:—
Cook 400g (1lb) fresh minced meat, onion, worcester sauce, nutmeg, breadcrumbs, and seasoning in stock until tender. Thicken with 5g (½oz) of flour.

Ingredients

1 onion, chopped
250g (½pt) stock
1–2 15ml (table) spoon worcester sauce
1 15ml (table) spoon breadcrumbs
pinch nutmeg
seasoning
300g (12oz) cooked minced meat
400g (1lb) cooked potato
25g (1oz) butter
½ egg, beaten

Cooking

Main oven temperature: 220°C
Time: 40–45 mins
Dish: ovenware dish
Shelf: middle
Second oven temperature: 200°C
Fan oven temperature: 200°C

Serves 4–6

Irish Stew

Method

1 Trim off surplus fat from meat, cut into pieces.
2 Place layers of meat, onion and potato in bottom of saucepan, lightly seasoning each time.
3 Add stock to come three quarters of the way up layers.
4 Cover and simmer until tender.
5 Serve, sprinkle with chopped parsley.

Ingredients

1kg (2lb) neck or breast of lamb or mutton
2 large onions, chopped
1kg (2lb) potatoes, sliced
seasoning
stock
parsley, chopped

Cooking

Cook for 1½–2 hrs

Serves 4–6

Stuffed Pork Chops

Method

1 Place sliced onions in dish. Prepare chops, place on onions, season.
2 Make up stuffing and spread over the chops. Dot with lard, cover with foil, do not seal.
3 Serve with apple sauce (page 35).

Ingredients

2 onions, sliced (optional)
4 pork chops
seasoning
sage and onion stuffing (page 72)
25g (1oz) lard

Cooking

Main oven temperature: 190°C
Time: 45–60 mins
Dish: ovenware dish
Shelf: middle
Second oven temperature: 170–180°C
Fan oven temperature: 170–180°C

Serves 4

Beefburgers

Method

1 Mix beef and onion together and add seasoning.
2 Roll into a long thick sausage and cut into 6–8 rounds.
3 If grilling, brush with melted butter otherwise fry.

Ingredients

400g (1lb) lean beef, finely minced
½ onion, chopped
seasoning
butter or oil

Variations

Any of the following additions may
be made:
50–100g (2–4oz) cheese, finely grated
1 5ml (tea) spoon mixed herbs
50g (2oz) mushrooms, chopped

Cooking

Cook for 4–6 mins
each side

Makes 6–8

Hungarian Goulash

Method

1 Toss the meat in the seasoned flour.
2 Lightly fry the onions and pepper in the fat or oil for 4 minutes.
3 Add the meat and fry until browned.
4 Add the paprika pepper and fry for about 1 minute.
5 Stir in the tomato purée, nutmeg, seasoning and flour and cook for a further 2–3 minutes.
6 Add the stock, quartered tomatoes and bouquet garni. Bring to the boil stirring all the time.
7 Transfer to an oven casserole dish and cook in a slow oven
8 Remove bouquet garni and stir in the red wine.
9 Serve with boiled potatoes.

Ingredients

400g (1lb) stewing steak, cut into cubes
3 15ml (table) spoon seasoned flour
2 medium sized onions, chopped
1 green pepper, deseeded and chopped
25g (1oz) fat or oil
2 5ml (tea) spoon paprika pepper
3 5ml (tea) spoon tomato purée
½ 5ml (tea) spoon grated nutmeg
seasoning
50g (2oz) flour
250–375ml (½–¾pt) stock
2 large tomatoes, skinned and quartered
bouquet garni
wine glass of red wine (optional)

Cooking

Main oven temperature: 150°C
Time: 1½–2 hrs
Dish: ovenware dish
Shelf: middle
Second oven
temperature: 140–150°C
Fan oven
temperature: 140°C

Serves 4

Hot Pot

Method

1 Cut meat into pieces, remove fat. Wash and skin
  kidney, soak in salt water for 5 minutes, cut into small pieces.
2 Fry carrots, onion, mushrooms and potatoes individually
  in dripping.
3 Brown meat in dripping.
4 Place ingredients in layers in a casserole, lightly seasoning
  each time; finish with a layer of potatoes.
5 Pour over the stock, cover and bake.
6 Remove the lid for the last 20 minutes to brown the potatoes.
7 When cooked, drain off liquor, blend the cornflour with a little
  liquor, add remainder, bring to the boil in a saucepan, stirring
  continually, cook for 3 minutes. Pour over hot pot.

Ingredients

500g (1lb 4oz) stewing steak or
middle neck of lamb
50g (2oz) kidney
2 carrots, sliced
1 onion, sliced
25g (1oz) mushrooms, sliced
500g (1¼lb) potatoes, sliced
15g (½oz) dripping
2 tomatoes, quartered
seasoning
250ml (½pt) stock
25g (1oz) cornflour

Cooking

Main oven temperature: 150°C
Time: 2–2½ hrs
Dish: ovenware dish
Shelf: middle
⌈ Second oven
  temperature: 140–150°C
  Fan oven
⌊ temperature: 140°C

Serves 4

Beef Olives

Method

1 If the meat has not been sliced by the butcher, cut carefully
  into thin slices about 10×8cm (4×3in.) and beat on
  board to flatten. Prepare the stuffing and spread on each
  piece of meat, roll up and secure with a piece of cotton or
  fine string.
2 Fry onion and carrot in fat, add the olives.
3 Place in ovenware dish, add seasoning, bay leaf, crumble stock
  cube and water. Cover and bake until tender.
4 To serve, remove the cotton or string, place olives on dish,
  thicken sauce with cornflour and pour over meat.

Ingredients

500g (1¼lb) rump steak
sage and onion stuffing (page 72)
1 onion, sliced
1 carrot, sliced
25g (1oz) fat
seasoning
1 bay leaf
1 stock cube
250ml (½pt) water
1 5ml (tea) spoon cornflour

Cooking

Main oven temperature: 150°C
Time: 1½–2 hrs
Dish: large shallow
ovenware dish
Shelf: middle
⌈ Second oven
  temperature: 140–150°C
  Fan oven
⌊ temperature: 140°C

Serves 4

Spaghetti Bolognese

Method

1 Fry the bacon in the butter for 2–3 minutes, add the onion and celery and fry for a further 5 minutes until browned.
2 Add the beef and mushrooms and fry until browned.
3 Add the tomato purée, wine, stock, seasoning and nutmeg.
4 Cover and simmer until the meat is tender and the liquid in the sauce is reduced. Adjust the seasoning.
5 Meanwhile cook the spaghetti in boiling salted water 12–15 minutes until soft, drain. Rinse under hot running water. Stir in a little olive oil.
6 Drain and serve in a heated dish with the sauce poured over. Serve the grated cheese in a separate dish.

Ingredients

200g (8oz) spaghetti
a little olive oil
parmesan cheese, grated to serve

For the sauce

50g (2oz) bacon, chopped
15g (½oz) butter
1 onion, chopped
1 stick celery, chopped
200g (8oz) minced beef, raw
100g (4oz) mushrooms, sliced
1 15ml (table) spoon tomato purée
glass red wine (optional)
250ml (½pt) beef stock
seasoning
nutmeg, grated

Serves 4

Ragoût of Kidneys

Method

1 Remove any fat and fine skin from the kidneys. Use scissors or sharp knife to cut out core of kidneys, then slice, and season.
2 Melt 25g (1oz) of the butter and fry kidney slices for 3–5 minutes.
3 Melt the other 25g (1oz) of butter and fry onion add the flour, then add the water and beef extract cubes. Stir until it boils.
4 Add the sliced mushrooms, tomato purée, paprika pepper and kidneys, simmer until cooked.

Serve on a bed of rice.

Ingredients

6 sheep's kidneys
seasoning
1 onion, chopped
50g (2oz) butter
25g (1oz) flour
125ml (¼pt) hot water
2 stock cubes
50g (2oz) button mushrooms, sliced
1 5ml (tea) spoon tomato purée
pinch paprika pepper

Cooking

Cook for 15–20 mins

Serves 2

Raised Pork Pie

Method

1 Mix pork with the onion. Add herbs, seasoning and enough stock to make the mixture moist.
2 Prepare the pastry, divide into a two third and one third portions, placing the one third portion in a covered basin in a warm position.
3 Using a well greased 18cm (7in.) tin with loose base. Roll out the pastry and fit into the tin pressing up the sides.
4 Place filling in the centre and cover with remaining pastry, press the edges together. Make a hole in the centre and brush with beaten egg.
5 Bake, after 1½ hours remove from tin and cook for a further 15–30 minutes.
6 Dissolve gelatine in stock and pour through hole in centre using a funnel. Leave to cool.

Variations
Raised Game Pie

1 Line the base and side of pie with sausagemeat.
2 Mix other meats together. Place in centre and continue as for pork pie.

Ingredients
1 onion, finely chopped
650g (1¾lb) lean pork, cut into cubes or minced
1 5ml (tea) spoon chopped sage or
½ 5ml (tea) spoon dried sage
seasoning
stock
300g (12oz) hot water crust pastry, (page 126)
egg, beaten
1½ 5ml (tea) spoon gelatin
125ml (¼ pt) stock

Ingredients
300g (12oz) sausage meat
100g (4oz) ham, chopped
150g (6oz) lean steak, minced
1 cooked pheasant or 2 pigeons, cut finely

Cooking
Main oven temperature: 190°C
Time: 1¾–2 hrs
Tin: 18cm (7in.) loose based cake tin
Shelf: middle
Second oven temperature: 170–180°C
Fan oven temperature: 170°C

Serves 4–5

Pork Chops with Sweet and Sour Sauce

Method

1 Grill the chops.
2 Fry the onion in the oil.
3 Add remaining ingredients, and simmer for 5 minutes.
4 Place chops on serving dish and cover with sauce.

Ingredients
4–6 pork chops
1 onion, chopped
1 15ml (table) spoon oil
400g (1lb) tinned pineapple, crushed with juice
1 15ml (table) spoon demerara sugar
1 15ml (table) spoon worcester sauce
juice 1 lemon
1 15ml (table) spoon vinegar
1 5ml (tea) spoon made mustard
seasoning

Serves 4–6

64

Crown Roast of Lamb

Method

This joint consists of two or three best ends of neck of lamb containing 14–18 cutlets, which adhere to each other at the bases, after the chine has been removed. The cutlets are trussed together into a circle to form a crown. The butcher will prepare this joint for you, with the exception of the filling or stuffing for the centre. To prevent burning, cover the ends of the cutlet bones with foil. When cooked place cutlet frills over ends of bones and garnish the dish with whole, cooked tomatoes.

See illustration at the front of this book.

Ingredients

2–3 best ends of neck of lamb
orange and herb stuffing (page 73)

Cooking

Main oven temperature: 190°C
Time: 1¼–1½ hrs
Tin: roasting tin
Shelf: middle
Second oven temperature: 180–190°C
Fan oven temperature: 180°C

Serves 5–6

Moussaka

Method

1 Lightly fry onions in the butter. Add the meat.
2 Add the tomatoes, tomato purée, stock and seasoning.
3 Dry the potato slices and fry in the oil until golden brown. Drain on kitchen paper.
4 Place a layer of potatoes in the bottom of a deep sided oven casserole dish and then a layer of meat mixture and continue like this ending with a layer of potatoes. Sprinkle on the wine.
5 Make a sauce with the butter or margarine, the flour and the milk. Remove from the heat and add the slightly beaten egg and cheese. Mix well and pour over the potatoes.
6 Sprinkle liberally with grated parmesan cheese and bake until the top is browned.

Note: The traditional dish uses aubergines in place of potatoes, in which case slice the aubergines and fry in butter.

Ingredients

200g (8oz) onions, chopped
25g (1oz) butter
400g (1lb) cooked minced lamb or beef
200g (8oz) tomatoes, peeled and quartered
2 15ml (table) spoon tomato purée
2 15ml (table) spoon stock or water seasoning
600g (1½lb) potatoes, peeled and sliced thinly
oil for frying
4 15ml (table) spoon white wine

For the sauce

15g (½oz) butter or margarine
15g (½oz) flour
250ml (½pt) milk
1 egg
25g (1oz) cheese, grated
parmesan cheese, grated
seasoning

Cooking

Main oven temperature: 200°C
Time: 40–50 mins
Dish: round ovenware dish
Shelf: middle
Second oven temperature: 180°C
Fan oven temperature: 180°C

Serves 4–6

E

Scandinavian Style Risotto

Method

1 Melt the butter in a heavy saucepan and lightly fry the vegetables without browning.
2 Add the rice and cook for 3–4 minutes until the rice has absorbed the butter and is slightly browned.
3 Pour in 250ml (½pt) stock and add raisins, seasoning and cook gently for 20–25 minutes, stirring occasionally and gradually adding remaining stock.
4 Add the gammon and pineapple to the risotto 5 minutes before the cooking time is up. Serve with green salad.

Ingredients

2 medium sized onions, chopped
1 stick celery, finely sliced
1 green pepper, deseeded and sliced
50g (2oz) butter
150g (6oz) patna rice
500ml (1pt) chicken stock
50g (2oz) seedless raisins
seasoning
200g (8oz) cooked gammon, diced
1 small tin pineapple pieces, drained

Serves 4–6

Veal Fricassée

Method

1 Melt butter, brown meat and add the flour. Cook for 2 minutes, add the stock, lemon juice and seasoning, stirring all the time. Cover and simmer for 1 hour.
2 Blanch the mushrooms and onions in boiling water for 5 minutes. Add to the veal and cook for a further 30 minutes.
3 Add the cream and egg yolk just before serving.

Garnish with bacon rolls, puff pastry crescents, and parsley.

Ingredients

40g (1½oz) butter
400g (1lb) stewing veal, cubed
25g (1oz) flour
500ml (1pt) stock
2 5ml (tea) spoon lemon juice
seasoning
100g (4oz) button mushrooms
4–5 small onions
1–2 15ml (table) spoon cream
1 egg yolk

Cooking

Time : 1½ hrs

Serves 4–5

Beef Curry

Method

1 Brown the meat in the margarine, remove from heat.
2 Prepare the curry sauce.
3 Add the meat and simmer until tender or cook in the oven. Season and add lemon juice.
4 Meanwhile cook rice in boiling salted water, until soft. Rinse under hot running water, drain well.
5 Serve curry with rice and a selection of accompaniments.

Note: Lamb or chicken may be used instead of beef.

Ingredients

400g (1lb) stewing steak, cubed
40g (1½oz) margarine
250ml (½pt) curry sauce (page 33)
seasoning
a few drops of lemon juice
100g (4oz) patna rice

Accompaniments

chutney; fresh coconut, grated; green or red peppers, sliced; spring onion, chopped; bombay duck; lemon, sliced

Cooking

Main oven temperature: 150°C
Time: 2–3 hrs
Dish: ovenware dish
Shelf: middle

Second oven temperature: 140–150°C
Fan oven temperature: 140°C

Serves 4

Casseroled Beef in Wine

Method

1 Toss meat in seasoned flour.
2 Fry onion and bacon in butter. Remove from pan and add meat, fry until brown.
3 Place in casserole add stock, wine, mushrooms, bouquet garni and fried ingredients. Cover and bake in oven.

Ingredients

400g (1lb) stewing steak, cubed
2 15ml (table) spoon seasoned flour
1 onion, sliced
100g (4oz) bacon, chopped
50g (2oz) butter
125ml (¼pt) stock
125ml (¼pt) red wine
50g (2oz) mushrooms, sliced
bouquet garni

Cooking

Main oven temperature: 150°C
Time: 2–3 hrs
Dish: ovenware dish
Shelf: middle

Second oven temperature: 130–140°C
Fan oven temperature: 130–140°C

Serves 3–4

Boeuf Strogonoff

Method

1 Cut meat into strips 6×25mm ($\frac{1}{4}$×1in.) toss in seasoned flour.
2 Fry thinly sliced onion and button mushrooms in butter for 2–3 minutes. Add the meat and fry for a further 5 to 6 minutes.
3 Add the nutmeg and sour cream and heat mixture through. Do not allow to boil. Adjust seasoning.

Variation

Pork Strogonoff

Use pork fillet or tenderloin instead of the steak. Add 200g ($\frac{1}{2}$lb) skinned, chopped, tomatoes before adding the sour cream.

Ingredients

1kg (2lb) rump or fillet steak
50g (2oz) seasoned flour
2 onions, thinly sliced
200g (8oz) button mushrooms, thinly sliced
100g (4oz) butter
nutmeg, grated
seasoning
250ml ($\frac{1}{2}$pt) sour cream

Serves 4–6

Cornish Pasties

Method

1 Roll out pastry into 1 large round or 2 smaller rounds.
2 Pile up potato on about half the pastry. Place onion on top of potato.
3 Cut meat into small pieces and place on top of onion. Add seasoning. A few pieces of turnip or potato should be placed on top to save the meat from drying.
4 Damp edges of pastry, fold over in semi circular shape and crimp edges (by pinching the pastry with the left hand and folding over with the right to form a rope like effect on the side of pastry).
5 Place on a baking tray, brush with beaten egg, cook at the higher temperature for 10–15 minutes and reduce the temperature for a further 30–40 minutes.

Ingredients

100g (4oz) short crust pastry (page 126)
potato, finely sliced
onion, finely chopped
100g (4oz) steak, chuck or skirt
turnip, finely sliced
seasoning
egg, beaten

Cooking

Main oven temperature:
220 and 180°C
Time: 40–55 mins
Tin: baking tray
Shelf: middle
Second oven temperature:
210 and 170°C
Fan oven temperature:
210 and 170°C

Serves 2

Chicken Risotto

Method

1 Melt the butter and fry the bacon or ham and the onions.
2 When the onions have started to cook add the remaining vegetables and cook for a few minutes.
3 **Add** the rice and stir until transparent. Add about 250ml ($\frac{1}{2}$pt) chicken stock, garlic, seasoning, and herbs.
4 Cook over a moderate heat, uncovered, until the stock is absorbed. Continue to cook adding more stock as required until rice is just soft.
5 Add the chicken, stir well and continue cooking until the liquids are absorbed.
6 Stir in some grated parmesan cheese and serve.

Note: White wine can replace 125ml ($\frac{1}{4}$pt) of the chicken stock if preferred.

Ingredients

25g (1oz) butter
50g (2oz) bacon or ham, chopped
2 small onions, chopped
1 stick celery, chopped
1 green pepper, deseeded and chopped
50g (2oz) mushrooms, sliced
200g (8oz) patna rice
375ml ($\frac{3}{4}$pt) chicken stock
1 clove garlic, crushed
seasoning
herbs, fresh chopped (e.g. marjoram, thyme, basil) or pinch mixed herbs
200g (8oz) cooked chicken, coarsely chopped
parmesan cheese, grated

Serves 4

Chicken Pie

Method

1 Fry onion and bacon gently in butter until cooked.
2 Blanch mushrooms and pepper in boiling water for 5 minutes.
3 Add all ingredients to the condensed soup and season.
4 Place in pie dish and cover with pastry. Brush with beaten egg.
5 Bake until golden brown.

Ingredients

1 small onion, chopped
100g (4oz) bacon or ham, chopped
25g (1oz) butter
200g (8oz) cooked chicken, chopped
100g (4oz) mushrooms, chopped
$\frac{1}{2}$ pepper, deseeded and chopped
1 15ml (table) spoon parsley, chopped
1 tin condensed celery soup
seasoning
200g (8oz) short crust pastry (page 126)
egg, beaten

Cooking

Main oven temperature: 200°C
Time: 30–45 mins
Dish: 180cm (7in.)
ovenware pie dish
Shelf: middle
[Second oven
  temperature: 190–200°C
  Fan oven
  temperature: 190°C]

Serves 4–5

Chicken Casserole

Method

1 Fry onion, in butter.
2 Blend cornflour and add to stock.
3 Place chicken joints in dish, add stock, and other ingredients. Cover with foil. Bake.
4 Place chicken on serving dish, strain sauce and pour over.

Ingredients

1 small onion, chopped
15g ($\frac{1}{2}$oz) butter
3 5ml (tea) spoon cornflour
500–750ml (1–1$\frac{1}{2}$pt) stock
4 joints chicken
1 5ml (tea) spoon mixed herbs
seasoning
2–3 15ml (table) spoon tomato purée

Cooking

Main oven temperature: 190°C
Time: 1–1$\frac{1}{2}$ hrs
Dish: large ovenware dish
Shelf: middle

Second oven
temperature: 180–190°C
Fan oven
temperature: 180°C

Serves 4

Duck in Pineapple

Method

1 Cut duck into portions, place in the roasting tin, brush well with cooking oil. Pour over the pineapple juice and red wine, add seasoning and garlic.
2 Cook, basting frequently with juices.
3 To make sauce, blend cornflour with the orange juice. Remove juices from roasting tin and heat, remove excess fat but make up liquid to 250ml ($\frac{1}{2}$pt) with water. Pour over cornflour, return to the pan and boil for 3 minutes.
4 Add chopped pineapple, raisins and grated orange rind, heat through again.

Ingredients

2$\frac{1}{2}$–3kg (5–6lb) duck
cooking oil
1 small tin pineapple
125ml ($\frac{1}{4}$pt) red wine
seasoning
1 clove garlic, crushed
15g ($\frac{1}{2}$oz) cornflour
1 orange, grated rind and juice
50g (2oz) raisins, chopped

Cooking

Main oven temperature: 190°C
Time: 1–1$\frac{1}{2}$ hrs
Tin: roasting tin
Shelf: middle

Second oven
temperature: 180–190°C
Fan oven
temperature: 180°C

Serves 4–6

Stuffings
Parsley and Thyme Stuffing

Method

1 Mix all dry ingredients together.
2 Bind together with egg and milk.

Use for lamb, veal or chicken.

Ingredients

100g (4oz) breadcrumbs
1 15ml (table) spoon suet
2 5ml (tea) spoon parsley, chopped
rind of ½ lemon, finely grated
½ 5ml (tea) spoon thyme
seasoning
50g (2oz) bacon, finely chopped
(optional)
egg, beaten
milk

Veal Forcemeat Stuffing

Method

1 Combine bacon, suet, breadcrumbs, herbs, and
  grated lemon rind.
2 Season and bind with beaten egg.

Use for veal or lamb.

Ingredients

50g (2oz) bacon, chopped
50g (2oz) suet, chopped
100g (4oz) breadcrumbs
1 15ml (table) spoon parsley, chopped
½ 5ml (tea) spoon mixed herbs
rind of ½ lemon, grated
seasoning
egg, beaten

Sweet Corn Stuffing

Method

1 Fry onion in butter, cook slowly. Add sweet corn and seasoning, fry for a further 4–5 minutes. Allow to cool.
2 Add parsley, rind and some of the lemon juice, season. Add breadcrumbs and egg to bind.

Use for chicken.

Ingredients

1 onion, chopped
25g (1oz) butter
1 tin sweet corn, drained
1 15ml (table) spoon parsley, chopped
1 lemon, grated rind and juice
seasoning
100g (4oz) breadcrumbs
egg, beaten

Sausage Stuffing

Method

1 Blend herbs and seasoning into sausage meat, add breadcrumbs and mix well.
2 Add egg to make a pliable consistency.

Use to stuff poultry or roll into balls, coat with flour and cook with the joint.

Ingredients

1 5ml (tea) spoon mixed herbs
½ 5ml (tea) spoon sage
1 5ml (tea) spoon thyme
1 5ml (tea) spoon parsley, chopped
seasoning
400g (1lb) sausage meat
100g (4oz) breadcrumbs
egg, beaten

Sage and Onion Stuffing

Method

1 Melt the butter and fry onions gently for about 10 minutes, until soft.
2 Remove from heat, add sage, breadcrumbs and seasoning. Cool and stir in the beaten egg to bind.

Use for pork.

Ingredients

50g (2oz) butter
400g (1lb) onions, chopped
2 5ml (tea) spoon dried sage
100g (4oz) breadcrumbs
seasoning
egg, beaten

Orange and Herb Stuffing

Method

Fry onion in butter until cooked, add other ingredients, mix well together.

Use for lamb, duck and poultry.

See illustration opposite page 1.

Ingredients

50g (2oz) onion, chopped
25–50g (1–2oz) butter
100g (4oz) breadcrumbs
1 15ml (table) spoon mixed herbs
1 orange, grated rind and juice
1 egg
seasoning

Chestnut Stuffing

Method

1 Boil chestnuts for 5 minutes in their shells, remove from water and shell.
2 Place nuts, stock and mace in saucepan, bring to the boil, simmer 30–40 minutes.
3 Sieve, stir in butter, sugar and seasoning. Use when cold.
4 To make a thicker stuffing add 100g (4oz) breadcrumbs and grated rind of a lemon.

Ingredients

400g (1lb) chestnuts
500ml (1pt) stock
a piece of mace
50g (2oz) butter
1 5ml (tea) spoon caster sugar
seasoning

Batters
Coating Batter

Method

1 Mix the flour and salt together, add the egg.
2 Beating well, gradually add all the liquid until smooth.

Ingredients

100g (4oz) plain flour
pinch of salt
1 egg
125ml ($\frac{1}{4}$pt) milk or milk and water mixed

Pouring Batter

Method

1 Mix the flour and salt together, add the egg.
2 Beating well, gradually add all the liquid until smooth.

Ingredients

100g (4oz) plain flour
pinch of salt
1 egg
250ml ($\frac{1}{2}$pt) milk or milk and
water mixed

Yorkshire Pudding

Method

1 Place lard in tin and heat in oven.
2 Pour batter, bake until golden brown and well risen.

Ingredients

250ml ($\frac{1}{2}$pt) pouring batter
25g (1oz) lard

Cooking

Main oven temperature: 230°C
Time: 35–40 mins
Tin: 23cm (9in.)
square tin
Shelf: top
Second oven
temperature: 220°C
Fan oven
temperature: 200–210°C
Serves 6–8

Individual Yorkshire Puddings

Method

1 Place a small knob of lard in each of patty tin sections, heat
in oven.
2 Pour a little batter in each section, bake until well risen and
golden brown.

Ingredients

250ml ($\frac{1}{2}$pt) pouring batter
25g (1oz) lard

Cooking

Main oven temperature: 230°C
Time: 20–25 mins
Tin: 2 12 section patty tins
Shelf: top and middle
Second oven
temperature: 210–220°C
Fan oven
temperature: 200–210°C
Makes approximately 18.

Vegetables & Salads

Vegetables, whether home grown, shop bought or commercially frozen, make delicious accompaniments to any meal. In this section we have included recipes for vegetable dishes which may be served at lunch or supper to make light but nourishing meals on their own. As an alternative to cooked vegetables, try the tomato and pepper or winter salad served with grilled chops or steak.

Vegetable Cooking Chart

Vegetables	Preparation	Method	Time
Asparagus	Wash the spears well and trim off the hard base of stalks. Tie in bundles.	Simmer the tied bundles gently in salted water in saucepan with lid on.	20–30 minutes until the green part of stalk is tender
Beans, broad	Shell and rinse in cold water.	250ml ($\frac{1}{2}$pt) of boiling salted water to a $\frac{1}{2}$kg (1lb). Boil rapidly.	10–25 minutes, according to size
Beans, butter (dried)	Wash and soak for 12–24 hours.	Drain, bring to the boil in cold salted water, simmer until tender	40 minutes to 1$\frac{1}{2}$ hours.
Beans, french	Top and tail the beans. String if necessary. Cut into 3 or 4 pieces if large, otherwise cook whole.	250ml ($\frac{1}{2}$pt) of boiling salted water to a $\frac{1}{2}$kg (1lb). Boil rapidly.	15–20 minutes
Beans, runner	Top, tail and string both sides. Slice beans transversely as thinly as possible.	250ml ($\frac{1}{2}$pt) of boiling salted water to a $\frac{1}{2}$kg (1lb). Boil rapidly.	10–20 minutes
Beetroot	Wash and scrub the beet, do not break skins.	Cold salted water to cover. Bring to the boil, simmer	From 30 min to 1$\frac{1}{2}$ hours according to size
Broccoli	Wash well, trim off hard leaves and stems.	Gently simmer in salted water. 250ml ($\frac{1}{2}$pt) to the $\frac{1}{2}$kg (1lb).	15–20 minutes
Brussels sprouts	Wash well and trim off outside leaves and cut off bottoms of stalks. Cut an incision in stalk.	Put prepared sprouts in boiling salted water, boil rapidly.	15–20 minutes
Cabbage	Remove outside leaves and cut in quarters. Cut the thick central stem from each piece. Cut into small pieces and wash in cold salted water. Drain and wash under tap.	Place in boiling salted water, boil rapidly.	10–15 minutes
Carrots (new)	Wash and remove skin by scrubbing.	Place in boiling salted water, boil rapidly.	15–20 minutes
Carrots (old)	Wash and peel off outer skin. Cut in slices.	Boil rapidly in salted water.	25–30 minutes

Vegetables	Preparation	Method	Time
Cauliflower	Cut off bottom of stem and outer leaves. Wash well. Cauliflower may be cooked whole or in sprigs.	Place stem downwards in boiling salted water to about half way up cauliflower.	Whole 20–30 minutes Sprigs 5–15 minutes
Celery	Remove any earth. Wash well and divide and scrub each stem. Trim off end of root. Cut off stringy and discoloured pieces.	Place in boiling salted water which just covers the celery.	25–30 minutes
Corn on cob	Strip outer musk and silk from cob. Trim stalk and rinse the cob.	Boiling unsalted water and boil rapidly.	8—12 minutes according to age of cob
Leeks	Cut off root, remove dark outer leaves and cut off most green from tops. Wash well. Cut down centre.	Place in boiling salted water just covering leeks. Simmer gently or steam in steamer.	15–20 minutes 30–35 minutes if steamed
Marrow Courgettes	Trim off stalk, peel and remove centre core. Cook whole or cut into pieces.	250ml ($\frac{1}{2}$pt) boiling salted water to $\frac{1}{2}$kg (1lb) marrow or courgettes.	15 minutes
Onions	Peel the outer skin away and cut off root and stalk end.	Put in cold salted water. Bring to boil and simmer gently.	15 minutes. Large 20–30 minutes
Parsnips	Wash well and peel. Cut in halves and quarters and wash again.	Put in cold salted water just to cover. Bring to the boil rapidly.	30–35 minutes
Peas	Shell and wash.	250ml ($\frac{1}{2}$pt.) boiling salted water with 1 5ml (tea) spoon sugar and sprig of mint, simmer gently.	10–15 minutes according to age and size
Potatoes (new)	Scrape and scrub lightly. Do not cut up unless very large.	Put in cold salted water. Add a sprig of mint and boil gently.	20–30 minutes
Potatoes (old)	Peel thinly as possible. Cut large ones in halves so that they are all about equal size and will take the same time for cooking.	Cold salted water, just to cover. Boil gently.	25–30 minutes
Spinach	Wash thoroughly to remove dirt and grit. Remove stalks and ribs from leaves.	25g (1oz) margarine melted in saucepan. Turn two to three times with a wooden spoon. Add salt after cooking.	7–10 minutes
Frozen vegetables		Cook according to instructions on packet.	

Baked Jacket Potatoes

Method

1 Scrub the potatoes, dry and prick well with a fork.
2 Brush with melted butter or wrap individually in foil. Place on baking tray. Bake until soft.
3 When cooked, cut in half and scoop out potato. Mash well with butter and seasoning. Replace filling, serve at once.

Variations for baked stuffed jacket potatoes

Follow the above method, but include one of the following variations:—

1 75g (3oz) cheese, grated
  25g (1oz) butter
  1 5ml (tea) spoon milk
  seasoning
2 75g (3oz) bacon, chopped and fried
  1 5ml (tea) spoon milk
  seasoning
3 2–3 15ml (table) spoon sour cream
  2 5ml (tea) spoon chives, chopped
  seasoning

Before serving, brush with milk or add a little cheese and grill until golden brown.

Ingredients

4 medium potatoes
butter
seasoning

Cooking

Main oven temperature: 200°C
Time: 1–1¼ hrs
Tin: baking tray
Shelf: middle/bottom

Second oven temperature: 190–200°C
Fan oven temperature: 190°C

Serves 4

Duchesse Potatoes

Method

1 Boil potatoes until tender, drain and dry over heat, sieve.
2 Melt butter in saucepan, add milk and potatoes, remove from heat, add eggs and grated nutmeg. Beat well together.
3 Pipe or fork into pyramids on a greased tray. Bake until golden brown and crisp.
   See illustration at front of book.

Ingredients

1kg (2lb) potatoes, prepared
50g (2oz) butter
125ml (¼pt) milk
2 eggs, beaten
nutmeg, grated

Cooking

Main oven temperature: 190°C
Time: 20–25 mins
Tin: baking tray
Shelf: top

Second oven temperature: 180–190°C
Fan oven temperature: 180°C

Makes 12

French Fried Potatoes

Method

1 Cut potatoes into strips 6mm ($\frac{1}{4}$in.) thick. Soak in cold water.

2 Heat oil or fat in deep fat pan. Dry the potatoes, then fry until soft. Remove from the fat, the potatoes can be kept for several hours in this condition.

3 When ready to serve, reheat fat and fry potatoes until crisp and golden brown. Drain well on kitchen paper and serve immediately.

Ingredients

1kg (2lb) potatoes, prepared
deep fat for frying

Serves 3–4

Roast Potatoes

Method

1 Cut potatoes into even sized pieces, wipe dry.

2 Place in melted fat or oil. Season and bake, turn during cooking to brown evenly.

Ingredients

1kg (2lb) potatoes, prepared
50g (2oz) dripping, lard or oil
seasoning

Cooking

Main oven temperature:
200–220°C
Time: 1–1$\frac{1}{2}$ hrs
Tin: roasting tin
Shelf: top

Second oven
temperature: 190–200°C
Fan oven
temperature: 180–190°C

Potatoes Lyonnaise

Method

1 Melt the butter and fry the onions until brown and crisp. Remove, place in a hot dish.

2 Slice the potatoes coarsely and fry until brown, drain well and mix with onions in the hot dish.

Ingredients

50g (2oz) butter
2 medium onions, finely sliced
8 potatoes, boiled,

Serves 3–4

Crisp Fried Onion Rings

Method

1 Dip onions in milk and then seasoned flour.
2 Cook in 12mm (½in.) of hot cooking oil, until golden brown.
3 Drain on kitchen paper. Serve at once.

Ingredients

400g (1lb) onions, sliced in rings
a little milk
50g (2oz) flour
seasoning
oil for frying

Serves 4

Stuffed Peppers

Method

1 Cut a slice from the top of the peppers, remove seeds and fibrous centre. Cook peppers with lids in boiling salted water for 5 minutes.
2 Place rice, bay leaf, saffron and seasoning in boiling stock. Cover pan, reduce heat and simmer until rice is cooked and stock absorbed.
3 Remove bay leaf, add sultanas and chopped ham.
4 Drain and fill peppers with prepared mixture, dot with butter, replace lid, place upright in dish. Add 125ml (¼pt) water.
5 Cover with foil and bake.

Ingredients

2 large peppers
50g (2oz) patna rice
½ bay leaf
pinch crumbled saffron (optional)
seasoning
250ml (½pt) stock
50g (2oz) sultanas
50g (2oz) ham, chopped
knob of butter

Cooking

Main oven temperature: 190°C
Time: 30–40 mins
Dish: ovenware dish
Shelf: top/middle

Second oven temperature: 180–190°C
Fan oven temperature: 180°C

Serves 2

Pease Pudding

Method

1 Wash peas well, remove any discoloured peas. Soak overnight.
2 Tie the peas loosely in a cloth. Place in saucepan with salt, ham bone and enough water to cover. Boil for 2–3 hours.
3 Remove bag, sieve or blend peas, add butter, egg, herbs and seasoning to taste.
4 Beat until well mixed, tie in floured cloth, boil for a further 30 minutes. Turn on hot plate to serve.

Ingredients

200g (8oz) split peas
pinch salt
1 ham bone
25g (1oz) butter
1 egg, beaten
1 5ml (tea) spoon mixed herbs
seasoning

Serves 4

Stuffed Marrow

Method

1 Prepare marrow, cut lengthwise in half, scoop out seeds. Place in boiling water and cook until tender, do not overcook. Drain.
2 Fry mushrooms and onions in butter until cooked.
3 Mix with minced meat, chopped ham, parsley, breadcrumbs, seasoning and egg.
4 Place lower half of marrow in dish, pile on stuffing, cover with remaining half and bake.

Ingredients

1 medium size marrow

Stuffing

50g (2oz) mushrooms, finely chopped
1 onion, finely chopped
25g (1oz) butter
200g (8oz) minced cooked beef
50g (2oz) ham, chopped
½ 5ml (tea) spoon parsley, chopped
40g (1½oz) breadcrumbs
seasoning
1 egg, beaten

Cooking

Main oven temperature: 200°C
Time: 30–35 mins
Dish: oblong ovenware
Shelf: top

Second oven
temperature: 190–200°C
Fan oven
temperature: 190°C

Serves 4

Cauliflower au Gratin

Method

1 Cook cauliflower, drain.
2 Make sauce and add half the cheese.
3 Place cauliflower in ovenware dish, coat with sauce, sprinkle with grated cheese and brown under the grill.

Ingredients

1 cauliflower
250ml (½pt) white coating sauce
(page 30)
75g (3oz) cheddar cheese, grated

Serves 3–4

Braised Celery

Method

1 Fry bacon and onions in melted butter until tender, add the celery, fry lightly for a few minutes.
2 Place onions, bacon, celery and the stock in a casserole dish, season, cover and braise.

Ingredients

2 rashers of bacon, chopped
2 small onions, chopped
25g (1oz) butter
1 2 heads of celery, sliced
seasoning
250ml (½pt) stock approx.

Cooking

Main oven temperature: 200°C
Time: 1¼–1½ hrs
Dish: ovenware dish
Shelf: middle

Second oven
temperature: 190–200°C
Fan oven
temperature: 190°C

Serves 4

Winter Salad

Method

1 Mix prepared vegetables and apple together.
2 Add salad cream to bind mixture.
3 Pile onto a dish and decorate with chopped walnuts.

Ingredients

4 sticks celery, chopped
1 cooked beetroot, diced
½ small onion, chopped
2 eating apples, cored and chopped
salad cream
walnuts, chopped

Serves 4–6

Tomato and Pepper Salad

Method

1 Place vegetables in dish, toss in vinaigrette dressing just before serving.
2 Decorate with chopped parsley.

Ingredients

400g (1lb) salad tomatoes, sliced
1 onion, sliced
2 green peppers, deseeded and sliced
french dressing (page 36)
parsley, chopped

Serves 4–6

Prawn Cucumbers

Method

1 Cut cucumber lengthwise. Scoop out centre, with a spoon and chop. Add prawns, chopped celery, tomato ketchup, salad cream and seasoning, mix together.
2 Fill cucumber boats. Place on bed of shredded lettuce.
3 Decorate dish with tomato and radish waterlilies.

Ingredients

1 cucumber
100g (4oz) prawns
2 sticks celery, chopped
2 5ml (tea) spoon tomato ketchup
3 15ml (table) spoon salad cream
seasoning
1 lettuce, shredded

Garnish

3 small tomatoes
6 radishes

Serves 4

Green Salad

Method

1 Select any two or more of the ingredients.
2 Just before serving toss lightly in a bowl with french dressing, adding some finely chopped onion if liked.
3 Sprinkle with any of the following, chopped fresh parsley, chives, mint, tarragon, or other herbs.

Ingredients

1 lettuce
cress
watercress
endive
chicory
cabbage, shredded
green pepper, deseeded and sliced
french dressing (page 36)
onion, finely chopped (optional)
fresh herbs—parsley, chives, mint, tarragon, chopped

Cauliflower Salad

Method

1 Trim cauliflower and break into sprigs, cook in boiling water for 3–6 minutes. Drain and allow to cool.
2 Toss in french dressing before serving.
3 This dish can be decorated with parsley or with crisp streaky bacon lightly crumbled over the top.

Ingredients

1 cauliflower
french dressing (page 36)
parsley   }
streaky bacon } optional

Potato Salad

Method

1 Cook potatoes in boiling salted water until just cooked, do not allow to go fluffy.
2 Drain, allow to cool slightly, cut potatoes into cubes. While still warm toss gently in french dressing. Leave to cool.
3 Coat in mayonnaise and season.
4 Decorate with chopped chives, or chopped parsley.

Ingredients

400g (1lb) potatoes, prepared
french dressing }
mayonnaise   } (page 36)
seasoning
parsley or chives (optional)

Orange Salad

Method

1 Remove skin and pith of the orange with a sharp knife. Cut into either side of the segments and remove in sections.
2 Place in shallow dish with tarragon and french dressing. Allow to stand.
3 Place on a bed of lettuce and serve with poultry or fish.

Ingredients

2 oranges, peeled
tarragon, chopped
french dressing (page 36)
1 lettuce

Serves 6–8

Russian Salad

Method

1 Cook vegetables in boiling water for 5 minutes.
2 Place in layers with other ingredients in a salad bowl, season each layer with salt and pepper and a pinch of sugar. Cover each layer with mayonnaise.
3 Decorate with olives and anchovies.

Ingredients

1 small cauliflower, cut into sprigs
4 15ml (table) spoon peas
4 15ml (table) spoon carrots, diced
4 15ml (table) spoon turnips, diced
3 potatoes, diced
a few lettuce leaves, shredded
3 gherkins, sliced
1 small beetroot, diced
50g (2oz) ham, diced
50g (2oz) shrimps, chopped
50g (2oz) smoked salmon
chopped (optional),
1 15ml (table) spoon capers, chopped
seasoning
sugar
mayonnaise (page 36)

Garnish

stuffed olives
anchovies

Serves 10–12

Sweets

Whichever sweet dish is chosen as the last course for a meal, like the first course, it should complement the main dish. There are so many recipes for sweets, that it would be impossible to include them all. In this section there is a range of sweets and puddings typical to the British kitchen, as well as some more unusual dishes which may be served as part of a formal dinner party.

Hot Sweets
Fruit Crumble

Method

1 Place fruit in a greased dish, add sugar.
2 Prepare topping by rubbing the fat into the flour and adding the sugar, nuts and lemon rind.
3 Sprinkle over the fruit. Bake.
4 Serve hot with custard or cream.

Ingredients

Topping

75g (3oz) butter or margarine
150g (6oz) plain flour
50g (2oz) sugar, caster or demarara
50g (2oz) nuts, chopped (optional)
rind ½ lemon, grated

Filling

400g (1lb) fruit (see below)
800g (2lb) if fruit has to be stoned
75–100g (3–4oz) sugar

e.g. plums, apricots, apples, rhubarb, gooseberries, cherries, raspberries.

Cooking

Main oven temperature: 220°C
Time: 40–50 mins
Dish: 1 litre (2pt) pie dish
Shelf: middle
Second oven temperature: 190–200°C
Fan oven temperature: 190°C

Serves 4–6

Baked Apples

Method

1 Core apples but do not peel.
2 Score the apples to allow them to swell without bursting.
3 Place them in a dish with a little water, fill the centre of each apple with a mixture of currants, brown sugar, and lemon juice.
4 Bake.

Ingredients

4 or 6 large cooking apples
brown sugar
currants
lemon juice

Cooking

Main oven temperature: 180°C
Time: 50–70 mins
Tin: baking trays
Shelf: middle
Second oven temperature: 160–170°C
Fan oven temperature: 160°C

Serves 4–6

Sponge Pudding

Method

1 Cream fat and sugar, add the eggs gradually, beating all the time.
2 Fold in the sieved flour and add a little milk to give a soft dropping consistency.
3 Add the flavour that is required (vanilla essence, orange or lemon juice).
4 Place mixture into a well greased basin. Cover with greased paper or aluminium foil.
5 Steam (refer to points 6 and 7, page 59).
6 Serve with jam sauce (page 34).

Ingredients

100g (4oz) butter
100g (4oz) caster sugar
2 eggs
150g (6oz) self raising flour
vanilla essence

Variations

add 75g (3oz) sultanas instead of flavouring
place 50g (2oz) jam or syrup in bottom of basin

Cooking

Time : 1½ hrs
Dish : 750ml (1½pt) pudding basin

Serves 4–6

Hot Vanilla Soufflé

Method

1 Melt butter in a saucepan, add flour, blend and cook gently for 1 minute.
2 Slowly add milk a little at a time, stirring well between each addition to produce a smooth sauce. Bring to the boil, stirring all the time.
3 Remove from the heat and add the sugar and vanilla, leave until cold.
4 Beat in egg yolks.
5 Whisk egg whites until stiff, fold into mixture.
6 Place in greased dish and bake.
7 Serve straight from the oven.

Ingredients

25g (1oz) butter
15g (½oz) plain flour
125ml (¼pt) milk
25g (1oz) caster sugar
vanilla essence
3 eggs

Cooking

Main oven temperature: 200°C
Time: 30–40 mins
Dish: 18cm (7in) soufflé dish
Shelf: middle
Second oven temperature: 180–190°C
Fan oven temperature: 180°C

Serves 3–4

Variations

Chocolate: 40g (1½oz) plain chocolate, melted, add after the egg yolks.
Orange or lemon: omit the vanilla essence, add the grated rind and juice of 2 lemons or 1½ oranges after the egg yolks.

Apple Charlotte

Method

1 Melt the butter and dip in the slices of bread.
2 Line the dish with bread leaving some for the top.
3 Stew apples with lemon; when half-cooked fill the dish with apples and half the brown sugar in layers.
4 Cover with the remaining bread, sprinkle on the rest of the sugar and any extra butter.
5 Cook until crisp.

Ingredients

125g (5oz) butter
slices of bread, crust removed
1kg (2lb) cooking apples, sliced
juice and rind of 1 lemon, grated
100g (4oz) brown sugar

Cooking

Main oven temperature: 200°C
Time: 30–40 mins
Dish: 1 litre (2pt) oval dish
Shelf: top/middle

Second oven temperature: 190°C
Fan oven temperature: 180°C

Serves 4–6

Christmas Pudding

Method

1 Place into a large bowl, the flour, breadcrumbs, salt, mixed spice, grated rinds of the orange and lemon, suet and sugar. Mix thoroughly.
2 Add all fruit, nuts, and grated carrot, stir very well.
3 Add the eggs to the mixture, followed by the orange and lemon juice and the brandy.
4 Mix to a soft dropping consistency with the milk or beer, or stout or barley wine.
5 Turn the mixture into greased pudding basins.
6 Cover with greaseproof paper and tie down. Cover the greaseproof paper with tin foil and seal down. Steam. (Refer to points 6 and 7, page 59).
7 Remove the coverings from the puddings and leave to cool. Cover with fresh greaseproof paper and store in a cool dry larder.
8 When required steam the puddings for a further 2–4 hours.

Ingredients

200g (8oz) plain flour
400g (1lb) fresh breadcrumbs
1 level 5ml (tea) spoon salt
2 level 5ml (tea) spoon mixed spice
1 orange, juice and grated rind
1 lemon, juice and grated rind
600g (1lb 8oz) suet, chopped
400g (1lb) brown sugar
400g (1lb) currants
400g (1lb) sultanas
200g (8oz) glacé cherries, quartered
50g (2oz) almonds, chopped
400g (1lb) raisins, stoned
100g (4oz) mixed peel
50g (2oz) ground almonds
600g (1lb 8oz) cooking apples, peeled and chopped
1 medium carrot, grated
8 standard eggs, beaten
1 wine glass brandy (optional) or milk, beer, stout, barley wine to mix

Cooking

Time: 6–8 hrs when made 2–4 hrs before serving
Dishes: Total of 3.5 litre (6pt) pudding basins

Fruit Pie

Method

1 Make up pastry (page 126).
2 Place fruit in dish with 2–4 15ml (table) spoon water (according to fruit) and sugar.
3 Roll out pastry a little larger than the dish, cut off a strip about 12mm ($\frac{1}{2}$in.) wide.
4 Damp and press this strip of pastry onto the edge of dish, damp again and cover with the remaining pastry. Trim and decorate edges. Make a small incision in top to allow steam to escape. Bake.

Note: Use a pie funnel if necessary.

Ingredients

300g (12oz) short crust pastry (page 126)
1kg (2lb) fruit, prepared
water
sugar to taste

Cooking

Main oven temperature: 220°C
Time: 40–45 mins
Dish: 1 litre (2pt) oval ovenware pie dish
Shelf: middle

Second oven temperature: 190–200°C
Fan oven temperature: 190°C

Serves 4–6

Queen of Puddings

Method

1 Infuse lemon in the milk, by heating the milk to blood temperature.
2 Strain into a bowl add butter and sugar.
3 When dissolved add the breadcrumbs mix and leave to cool.
4 Add yolks, mix thoroughly, turn into a greased dish.
5 Stand for 30 minutes, bake in a water bath until set.
6 Cool slightly, spread with jam, make up meringue as for lemon meringue pie (page 96), pipe on top of pudding.
7 Dust with caster sugar and place in oven to brown meringue.

Ingredients

Base
rind of 1 lemon, thinly pared
250ml ($\frac{1}{2}$pt) milk
15g ($\frac{1}{2}$oz) butter
25g (1oz) sugar
75g (3oz) breadcrumbs
2 egg yolks
jam

Meringue
100g (4oz) caster sugar
2 egg whites
caster sugar

Cooking

Main oven temperature: 190°C
Time: 30–45 mins base, 15 mins meringue
Dish: 750ml ($\frac{3}{4}$pt) oval ovenware in roasting tin of water
Shelf: middle

Second oven temperature: 170–180°C
Fan oven temperature: 170–180°C

Serves 4

Bread and Butter Pudding

Method

1 Butter bread, remove crusts and cut in half diagonally.
2 Wash fruit, place between layers of bread in the dish.
3 Mix eggs, sugar and essence together and add the milk gradually. Pour over the bread. Bake.

Ingredients

50g (2oz) butter
6 small slices bread
100g (4 oz) currants and sultanas
2 eggs, beaten
50g (2oz) caster sugar
vanilla essence
250ml ($\frac{1}{2}$pt) milk

Cooking

Main oven temperature: 180°C
Time: 55–65 mins
Dish: 1 litre (2pt) oval ovenware
Shelf: middle

Second oven temperature: 160–170°C
Fan oven temperature: 160°C

Serves 4–6

Baked Custard

Method

1 Mix milk with sugar, warm gently until dissolved. Cool to blood heat, pour onto lightly beaten eggs. Mix in vanilla essence.
2 Strain into a lightly greased dish, sprinkle with grated nutmeg.
3 Place in a water bath. Bake.

Ingredients

500ml (1pt) milk
50g (2oz) sugar
3 eggs
vanilla essence
nutmeg, grated

Cooking

Main oven temperature: 180°C
Time: 50–60 mins
Tin: 1 litre (2pt) oval ovenware, in a roasting tin of water
Shelf: middle

Second oven temperature: 160–170°C
Fan oven temperature: 160°C

Serves 4–6

Syrup Tart

Method

1 Make up pastry (page 126). Line plate, re-roll trimmings, cut into strips 12mm ($\frac{1}{2}$in.) wide for decoration.
2 Mix breadcrumbs and lemon rind with syrup. Pour filling into lined plate. Place strips of pastry lattice fashion over filling. Pinch up edges. Bake.

Variations

Lemon curd and coconut—mix 25g (1oz) coconut with 200g (8oz) lemon curd.
Apricot jam and chopped nuts—mix 25g (1oz) nuts, chopped, with 200g (8oz) apricot jam.

Ingredients

200g (8oz) short crust pastry (page 126)

Filling

300g (12oz) golden syrup
50g (2oz) white breadcrumbs
rind of $\frac{1}{2}$ lemon, finely grated

Cooking

Main oven temperature: 200°C
Time: 30–35 mins
Dish: 25cm (10in.) ovenware plate
Shelf: top

Second oven temperature: 190°C
Fan oven temperature: 180°C

Serves 6–8

Sweet Pancakes

Pouring Batter (page 74)

Method

1 Prepare a 15cm (½in.) thick based frying pan by melting a little butter in it and coating the base and sides. Pour off the excess butter.
2 Pour a little batter into the pan and cover the base completely.
3 Cook until golden brown underneath, turn with a palette knife. Cook second side. Use according to the recipe.

Fillings

Lemon. Add grated lemon rind to batter. Sprinkle lemon juice and caster sugar over the cooked pancake.

Ginger and banana. Put a 5ml (tea) spoon ginger in with the flour. Mash 1 banana, per person, with double cream. Spread over pancakes.

Almond and apricot. Simmer 50g (2oz) dried apricots in a little water and sugar to taste with a good squeeze of lemon. When they are soft add 25g (1oz) almonds, chopped. Fill pancakes, serve with cream.

Cream cheese. Whip 200g (8oz) cream cheese, 1 egg, 15ml (table) spoon sugar and vanilla essence together. Spread filling over pancakes, fold in half and half again. Fry again for 2–3 minutes in butter. Serve with raspberries, strawberries, pineapple, mandarin oranges etc.

Fruit Fritters

Method

1 Make up coating batter (page 73).
2 Dry fruit and dip in batter to coat evenly. Fry in deep fat. Drain.
3 Sprinkle with caster sugar and serve hot or cold.
Rum may be sprinkled over the fruit before coating.

Ingredients

coating batter (page 73)
apple, sliced and soaked in lemon juice
banana, sliced
orange segments
pineapple pieces
oil for frying
caster sugar
rum (optional)

Adjust quantities to personal requirements

Rice Pudding

Method

1 Place the rice, butter and sugar in an ovenware dish.
2 Add the vanilla to milk and pour over rice. Sprinkle nutmeg on top.
3 Cook slowly.

Variations

1 Orange or lemon rice: Infuse the rind of 1 lemon or orange into the milk before cooking the rice pudding. Omit the nutmeg. After the pudding has been cooking for $1\frac{1}{2}$ hrs remove from the oven, cool for 10 mins and then stir in beaten egg. Return to the oven and then cook for a further 15 mins. When cooked, chill and serve cold.
2 Caramelised rice: Dissolve 50g (2oz) sugar in 4 15ml (table) spoon water, boil gently until it turns golden brown. Remove from heat and stir in milk. Pour over rice, add an extra 5ml (tea) spoon sugar. Serve hot or cold.
3 Fruit rice: 25–50g (1–2oz) glacé cherries, sultanas, or currants may be added to rice.

Ingredients

50g (2oz) carolina rice
25g (1oz) butter
50g (2oz) sugar
vanilla essence
500ml (1pt) milk
nutmeg

Cooking

Main oven temperature: 160°C
Time: 2 hrs approx.
Dish: 1 litre (2pt) oval ovenware
Shelf: middle
[Second oven temperature: 140–150°C
Fan oven temperature: 140°C]

Serves 4–6

Casserole of Fruit

Method

1 Drain fruit. Place in dish with sugar, water and lemon rind. Cover with lid or foil. Bake.
2 When cooked remove lemon rind. Serve with cream.

Ingredients

100g (4oz) dried apricots ⎫ soaked
100g (4oz) dried prunes ⎭ overnight
25–50g (1–2oz) sugar
125–250ml ($\frac{1}{4}$–$\frac{1}{2}$pt) water
rind of $\frac{1}{2}$ lemon, cut into strips

Cooking

Main oven temperature: 190°C
Time: $1\frac{1}{4}$–$1\frac{1}{2}$ hrs
Dish: 1 litre (2pt) round ovenware
Shelf: top/middle
[Second oven temperature: 170–180°C
Fan oven temperature: 170°C]

Serves 4

Eve's Pudding

Method

1 Prepare topping as for victoria sandwich, (page 109) add milk to make a softer mixture.
2 Prepare fresh fruit, add sugar.
3 Place fruit in greased dish.
4 Put sponge mixture on top. Bake.
5 Serve hot with custard or cream.

Ingredients

Topping

75g (3oz) butter or margarine
75g (3oz) caster sugar
1 egg
100g (4oz) self raising flour
2–3 15ml (table) spoon milk

Filling

400g (1lb) fruit e.g. apples, plums, rhubarb, gooseberries, blackberries, pineapple, peaches, tinned or fresh
sugar to taste

Cooking

Main oven temperature: 190°C
Time: 40–50 mins
Dish: 1 litre (2pt) oval ovenware
Shelf: middle

Second oven temperature: 170–180°C
Fan oven temperature: 170°C

Serves 4–5

Cold Sweets
Dutch Apple Tart

Method

1 Prepare flan pastry. Line tin.
2 Mix apple, lemon, almonds, sultanas, and sugar.
3 Spread raspberry jam over the flan base, fill with apple mixture.
4 Make a lattice design over the mixture with strips of pastry.
5 Bake.
6 Serve hot or cold, with cream.

See illustration opposite page 112.

Ingredients

150g (6oz) sweet flan pastry (page 127)
400g (1lb) apples, grated
1 lemon, juice and grated rind
50g (2oz) almonds, coarsely chopped
50g (2oz) sultanas
sugar to taste
raspberry jam

Cooking

Main oven temperature: 200°C
Time: 30–40 mins
Tin: 20 × 20cm (8 × 8in.)
Shelf: middle

Second oven temperature: 190°C
Fan oven temperature: 180°C

Serves 4–6

Sponge Fruit Flan

Method

1 Prepare tin as for sponge sandwich (page 106).
2 Make up mixture as for swiss roll (page 112). Bake.
3 Allow to cool slightly and remove from tin.
4 When flan is cold, arrange fruit in centre. Make arrowroot glaze and pour over fruit.

Ingredients

swiss roll mixture (page 112)
fruit
arrowroot glaze (page 35)

Cooking

Main oven temperature: 200°C
Time: 15–20 mins
Tin: 23cm (9in.) sponge flan tin
Shelf: top

Second oven temperature: 190–200°C
Fan oven temperature: 190°C

Serves 6–8

Apple Strudel

Method

1 Place flour and salt in bowl, make a well in centre. Add eggs, oil and lemon juice. Beat together until dough leaves bowl clean. Cover and leave in a warm place for 30 minutes.
2 Roll paste out on a floured board until thin. Place on a floured cloth and spread out thinly into a rectangle. Trim edges lightly, brush with oil.
3 Prepare the ingredients for the filling, soak the breadcrumbs in the melted butter.
4 Spread jam over the pastry; then the soaked breadcrumbs, apple and grated lemon, sultanas, almonds, and finally sugar and cinnamon.
5 Fold 25mm (1in.) over the shorter sides and then roll up lengthwise.
6 Brush with oil, bake. Dust with icing sugar.

Ingredients

200g (8oz) flour
pinch of salt
2 eggs
2 15ml (table) spoon oil
juice 2 lemons

Filling

1 15ml (table) spoon cooking oil
50g (2oz) fresh breadcrumbs
50g (2oz) butter, melted
100g (4oz) strawberry jam, sieved
1kg (2lb) apples, shredded
rind of 2 lemons, grated
75g (3oz) sultanas
100g (4oz) ground almonds
75g (3oz) brown sugar
2 5ml (tea) spoon cinnamon

Cooking

Main oven temperature: 200°C
Time: 20–30 mins
Tin: large baking tray
Shelf: middle

Second oven temperature: 180–190°C
Fan oven temperature: 180°C

Serves 4–6

Cream Cheese Strudel

Method

1. Make strudel paste as for apple strudel.
2. Work in the creamed butter and sugar gradually into the cheese, add egg and vanilla, beating thoroughly.
3. Drain sultanas and add to the cream cheese mixture with the lemon rind.
4. Roll and pull the strudel paste as for apple strudel, brush or dab with melted butter and sprinkle well with the crumbs. Put the mixture on in small pieces, then finish as for apple strudel.

Ingredients

Strudel paste as for apple strudel, (page 94)

Filling

250g (10oz) cream cheese, sieved
40g (1½oz) butter
50g (2oz) caster sugar
1 small egg
vanilla essence
65g (2½oz) sultanas, soaked overnight in water and 1 5ml (tea) spoon lemon juice
a little lemon rind, grated
25–50g (1–2oz) butter, melted
browned crumbs
icing sugar

Cooking

Main oven temperature: 200°C
Time: 20–30 mins
Tin: large baking tray
Shelf: middle

Second oven temperature: 180–190°C
Fan oven temperature: 180°C

Serves 4–6

Creme Caramel

Method

1. *Caramel:* Place sugar and water in a small saucepan. Leave until sugar is dissolved.
2. Bring to the boil. Allow to boil quickly (do not stir) until mixture turns pale brown. Remove at once.
3. Pour caramel into greased basin. Move gently until base and sides are coated, leave until quite cold.
4. *Creme:* Beat eggs, stir into milk. Add sugar and vanilla essence.
5. Pour into prepared basin. Cover with foil or greased greaseproof paper. Steam, (refer to points 6 and 7 page 59).

To serve: Run a knife round the sides of the basin and invert onto serving dish.

Ingredients

Caramel

100g (4oz) sugar
125ml (¼pt) water

Creme

3 eggs
250ml (½pt) milk
25g (1oz) caster sugar
½ 5ml (tea) spoon vanilla essence

Cooking

Time: 30–40 mins
Dish: ½–¾ litre (1–1¼pt) basin

Serves 3–4

Lemon Meringue Pie

Method

1 Make up pastry (page 126), roll out and line tin, bake blind (page 12).
2 Place sugar, butter, water, lemon juice and rind into a saucepan. Heat, stirring until the sugar has dissolved. Cool.
3 Blend cornflour with a little milk, add remainder, stir into the heated mixture and bring to the boil. Continue to stir until the mixture has thickened. Cool slightly.
4 Beat egg yolks and pour into the thickened mixture. Pour into pastry case.
5 Whisk egg whites until stiff. Add half the sugar and continue whisking. Fold in remaining sugar. Use to cover lemon mixture, bake.

Ingredients

250g (10oz) short crust pastry (page 126)

Filling

65g (2½oz) caster sugar
40g (1½oz) butter
125ml (¼pt) water
25g (1oz) cornflour
125ml (¼pt) milk
3 egg yolks
2 lemons, juice and finely grated rind

Meringue

3 egg whites
100g (4oz) caster sugar

Cooking

Main oven temperature: 200°C for pastry; 180°C for meringue
Time: 20–30 mins for pastry, 15–20 mins for meringue
Tin: 18 × 30cm (7½ × 11½in.) swiss roll tin
Shelf: top/middle

Second oven temperature: 190 and 170°C
Fan oven temperature: 190 and 170°C

Serves 6–8

Raspberry Cream

Method

1 Reserve a few of the raspberries for decoration and then sieve or purée the remaining raspberries and the juice.
2 Melt the jelly in 125ml (¼pt) water and add the raspberry purée. Make up to 500ml (1pt) with ice cubes.
3 Stir continuously and when the jelly is on the point of setting remove the ice cubes and whisk jelly vigorously whilst gradually adding the evaporated milk.
4 Pour into a glass dish and place in the refrigerator to set.
5 Decorate with the whipped cream and the reserved raspberries.

Ingredients

1 small tin raspberries
1 raspberry jelly
1 small tin evaporated milk
1 125ml (¼pt) carton double cream
ice cubes

Serves 4–6

Cold Soufflé

In this recipe ingredients have been grouped for each stage of preparation.

Method

1 Prepare a 13cm (5in.) soufflé dish, see below, place all ingredients into a bowl over hot water. Whisk together until thick and creamy and lighter in colour. Remove from over hot water, whisk until cool.

2 Put fruit syrup into a basin over warm water, add the gelatine and warm gently until dissolved, allow to cool slightly. Add to stage 1 mixture, pouring slowly from a height in a steady stream.

3 Add purée and fold in cream mix evenly.

4 Stiffly whisk egg whites, mix in evenly, do not over mix. Turn into dish and allow to set.

5 Remove the greaseproof collar, using a hot, wet, wide bladed knife to ease it away from the edge. Decorate the side of the soufflé with chopped nuts, cake crumbs or coconut. Pipe cream around edge. Decorate centre with small pieces of fruit.

Variations

Fresh fruit

Use fresh cooked fruit instead of tinned. Use lemon juice instead of fruit syrup in stages 1 and 2.

Lemon, orange

Grated rind and juice of 3 lemons, 1½ oranges or 3 tangerines in stage 1 and 125ml (¼pt.) double cream to make up the weight of purée in stage 3. Decorate with crystallized fruit on top.

Preparation of souffle dish

Cut a double piece of greaseproof long enough to go round the souffle dish and overlap, and 8cm (3in.) wider than the depth of the dish. Fix closely around the dish and secure. It should be tight enough around the rim of the dish to prevent the mixture dripping through. When the mixture is poured in the dish it will rise about 25cm. (1in.) above the top of the dish.

See illustration opposite page 112.

Ingredients

1 3 egg yolks
75g (3oz) caster sugar
1 15ml (table) spoon lemon juice
2 15ml (table) spoon canned fruit syrup

2 2 level 5ml (tea) spoon gelatine
2 level 5ml (tea) spoon fruit syrup

3 125ml (¼pt) canned fruit purée. Raspberry, strawberry, apricot, etc. using tinned fruit
250ml (½pt) double cream, whipped

4 3 egg whites

5 toasted coconut, cake crumbs or nuts, finely chopped
double cream, whipped

Crystallized Fruit Meringue

Method

1 Draw 3 18cm (7in.) circles on greaseproof paper, place onto baking trays and grease well.
2 Make meringue (page 116), place in a piping bag (which has a 18mm (¾in.) star pipe in it).
3 Following the circle drawn on the greaseproof paper, pipe a circle of meringue. Continue in decreasing circles until the centre is completely filled in. Repeat with the second circle. For the third circle pipe rosettes around the outside and then pipe lines across one way and then the other to form a lattice design. Dry out as for meringues.
4 When dry remove from the greaseproof paper. Fill with whipped cream and crystallized fruit, decorating the top by placing fruit in between the lattice design.

Ingredients

Meringue

6 egg whites
150g (6oz) caster sugar

Filling

250ml (½pt) double cream
200g (8oz) crystallized fruit

Cooking

Main oven temperature: 100°C
Time: 2½–3 hrs
Tin: baking trays
Shelf: top and middle
Second oven temperature: 90°C
Fan oven temperature: 90°C

Serves 4–6

Lemon Surprise

Method

1 Cream butter and sugar together, then add lemon rind. Beat until light and fluffy.
2 Add egg yolks, beating well. Stir in milk, lemon juice and flour.
3 Whisk eggs stiffly, fold in mixture and pour into greased dish.
4 Stand dish in roasting tin.
5 Cook until firm to the touch.

Ingredients

1 lemon, juice and rind, grated
50g (2oz) butter
100g (4oz) sugar
2 eggs, separated
250ml (½pt) milk
50g (2oz) self raising flour

Cooking

Main oven temperature: 200°C
Time: 40–45 mins
Tin: 1½ litre (2½pt) ovenproof dish in roasting tin with water
Shelf: top/middle
Second oven temperature: 180–190°C
Fan oven temperature: 170–180°C

Serves 4

Cheese Cake

Method

1 Make pastry up as for short crust pastry and line the flan ring.
2 Mix the margarine and sugar together, add the beaten egg, cheese, peel, currants, grated lemon rind and vanilla essence.
3 Mix thoroughly and fill prepared flan ring. Decorate the flan with pastry strips and brush with beaten egg. Bake. Serve cold.

Drained mandarin oranges may be placed on top of the cheese cake just before serving.

Ingredients

Pastry

200g (8oz) flour
pinch salt
100g (4oz) butter
40g (1½oz) sugar
milk and water
1 egg

Filling

50g (2oz) margarine
25g (1oz) caster sugar
1 egg
250g (10oz) curd cheese
25g (1oz) mixed peel
25g (1oz) currants
lemon rind, grated
2 drops vanilla essence
egg, beaten

Cooking

Main oven temperature: 180°C
Time: 40–50 mins
Tin: 23cm (9in.) flan ring
Shelf: middle

Second oven temperature: 170–180°C
Fan oven temperature: 170°C

Serves 6–8

Strawberry Shortbread

Method

1 Make up shortbread mixture (page 123). Divide mixture between two tins, smooth over and prick, cook, allow to cool.
2 Keeping some of the best strawberries to decorate top, slice the rest into a bowl, add sugar and half the whipped cream.
3 Fill the shortbread. Pipe cream on top and decorate with whole strawberries.

Ingredients

250g (10oz) shortbread mixture (page 123)

Filling

400g (1lb) strawberries, hulled
100g (4oz) caster sugar
250ml (½pt) double cream ⎱ whipped
15g (½oz) caster sugar ⎰ together

Cooking

Main oven temperature: 150°C
Time: 55–65 mins
Tin: 2 20cm (8in.) victoria sandwich tins
Shelf: middle

Second oven temperature: 140–150°C
Fan oven temperature: 140°C

Serves 4–6

Spicy Apple Cake

Method

1 Place prepared apples in a saucepan with 25g (1oz) of the butter or margarine, the lemon juice, sugar and mixed spice.
2 Cook gently until the apples are soft. Add the currants and the mixed peel, and leave to cool slightly.
3 Mix the grated lemon rind and cake crumbs together. Melt the remaining 75g (3oz) butter or margarine and gradually pour onto the crumbs, stirring continually.
4 Grease tin. Place a layer of the crumb mixture on the bottom, press down lightly and then a layer of the apple mixture. Repeat the layers, finishing with a layer of the crumb mixture.
5 Sprinkle the demerara sugar over the top and bake. Leave to cool slightly before removing from the tin. Serve hot with cream as a sweet or cold as a cake.

Ingredients

600g (12oz) cooking apples, sliced
100g (4oz) butter or margarine
juice 2 lemons
100g (4oz) caster sugar
1 5ml (tea) spoon mixed spice
40g (1½oz) currants
40g (1½oz) mixed peel
rind of 2 lemons, grated
400g (1lb) cake crumbs
1 10ml (dessert) spoon demerara sugar

Cooking

Main oven temperature: 190°C
Time: 25–35 mins
Tin: 20cm (8in.) round loose based cake tin
Shelf: middle
Second oven temperature: 180–190°C
Fan oven temperature: 180°C

Serves 6–8

Fruit Fool

Method

1 Stew the fruit in a very little water with the sugar (unless tinned or frozen fruit is used).
2 Sieve or purée the fruit.
3 Fold the purée into the custard and cream, add a few drops of lemon juice and extra sugar if necessary. Add colouring if required.
4 Turn into sundae dishes or other small dishes, place in refrigerator to chill.
5 Decorate with chopped nuts and serve with shortbread or sponge fingers.

See illustration opposite page 112.

Ingredients

400g (1lb) fruit
sugar to taste
125ml (¼pt) custard, ready made
125ml (¼pt) double cream
lemon juice
colouring (optional)
nuts, chopped

Makes 4

Icings

A simple sponge cake or victoria sandwich can be easily made into a party gâteau by decorating with icing and some fresh fruit. In this section there is the basic recipe for butter icing with some variations, and also the methods for making almond paste, royal icing and quick fondant icing for decorating a rich Christmas or birthday cake.

Butter Icing

Method

1 Cream butter, add sieved icing sugar, a little at a time, beating well.
2 Add flavouring desired. Beat well.

Basic Ingredients

400g (1lb) icing sugar, sieved
200g (8oz) butter

Glacé Icing

Method

1 Place sieved icing sugar in a bowl.
2 Add extra ingredients, according to the flavour required.
3 Add enough warm water to form a stiff coating consistency.
4 Use as required.

Basic Ingredients

400g (1lb) icing sugar, sieved
warm water

Variations on glacé icing and butter icing recipes

Almond: A few drops of almond essence.
Chocolate: 50g (2oz) cocoa (mixed with 1 15ml (table) spoon of warm water to form a paste), 25g (1oz) melted margarine.
Coffee: 2 level 5ml (tea) spoon instant coffee (dissolved in 2 5ml (tea) spoon warm water).
Lemon or orange: The grated rind and juice from half a lemon or orange. Orange or lemon colouring.

Quick Fondant Icing

Method

1 Slightly whisk egg whites.
2 Beat egg whites, glucose, glycerine and lemon juice with icing sugar until stiff consistency is obtained.
3 Knead well with cornfloured hands.
4 Use as required.

Ingredients

400g (1lb) icing sugar, sieved
1 egg white
1 15ml (table) spoon liquid glucose
1 5ml (tea) spoon glycerine
1 5ml (tea) spoon lemon juice

Almond Paste

Method

Sufficient to cover 20cm (8in.) round cake.

1 Whisk eggs and essence together. Whisk in sugar.
2 Stir in ground almonds. Adjust consistency by adding a little extra egg or ground almonds until mixture resembles a pliable dough, but is not sticky. Knead well.

If not required to be used at once, wrap well in waxed paper and keep in a cool place.

Ingredients

2 eggs
orange flower water
almond essence
200g (8oz) icing sugar
200g (8oz) caster sugar
400g (1lb) ground almonds

Royal Icing

Method

1 Place the egg whites, lemon juice and glycerine in a mixing bowl, gradually mix in icing sugar. Beat well until mixture is white.

Adjust consistency

1 If required for piping add more sieved icing sugar. The icing should stand in peaks.
2 If required to coat a large cake, add a little more liquid if necessary until a spreadable consistency is obtained.
3 Use at once, or if required to be left for a short time, cover bowl with a damp cloth.

Ingredients

200g (8oz) icing sugar, sieved
$1-1\frac{1}{2}$ egg whites
1 5ml (tea) spoon lemon juice
1 5ml (tea) spoon glycerine

Chocolate Fudge Icing

Method

1 Place the butter, sugar, liquid cocoa and milk in a saucepan and put on low heat.
2 Stir until butter and sugar melts, bring to the boil, boil briskly for 3 minutes.
3 Remove from the heat, add icing sugar and mix well, add warm water, vanilla essence and beat well for 5 minutes.
4 Pour over cake while still warm as this icing sets when cold.

For cake recipe see page 113.

Ingredients

25g (1oz) butter
50g (2oz) soft brown or demerara sugar
15g (½oz) cocoa (mix into paste with 3 15ml (table) spoon water)
2 5ml (tea) spoon milk
200g (8oz) icing sugar, sieved
2 15ml (table) spoon of warm water
vanilla essence

Peppermint Chocolate Icing

Method

1 Warm chocolate and water in a small saucepan over a low heat until dissolved.
2 Pour onto butter and sugar and beat until smooth.
3 Add peppermint essence to taste.

Ingredients

50g (2oz) plain chocolate
2 15ml (table) spoon water
25g (1oz) butter
150g (6oz) icing sugar, sieved
3 drops peppermint essence

Cakes

There are a variety of ways to make cakes but to ensure good flavour, texture and appearance it is necessary to take care and time over the initial preparation in order to obtain a successful home-baked cake. The choice, weighing and mixing of the correct ingredients and the careful preparation and lining of the tin will help you to produce a cake worthy to grace any table.

Preparation of Tins

Bun or patty tins

Lightly grease, using melted fat or oil.

Sandwich tins

Cut a disc of greaseproof paper to fit the base, grease paper and sides of tin with melted fat or oil.

Sandwich tins for sponge mixtures

Grease tin well with melted fat or oil. Sprinkle with an equal quantity of flour and caster sugar. This method is also used for a sponge flan tin.

Swiss roll tin

Cut a piece of greaseproof paper 2.5cm (1in.) larger all over than the tin. Make a short cut 2.5cm (1in.) from each end along the short sides. Place the paper in the tin, grease very well, using melted fat or oil. Tuck the cut corners in neatly.

Deep round

Cut a greaseproof paper circle to fit the base of the tin, also a strip for the sides 2.5cm (1in.) deeper than the cake tin. Taking the long strip, make a 13mm ($\frac{1}{2}$in.) fold along the edge, make cuts at intervals, cutting up to the fold line. Place this strip around the side of the tin (the folded cut portion fits into the base and forms pleats) lay the circle in the base. Grease well with melted fat or oil.

Deep square

Cut two pieces of greaseproof paper, the width of the tin and the length to equal base plus sides. Place one piece in one direction and the other in the opposite direction. Grease well with melted fat or oil.

Basic Methods

Rubbed in—scones, plain cakes etc.

In which the fat is rubbed into the flour. This type is economical to make, but becomes stale after a day or so, due to low fat content.

Creamed—rich cakes, victoria sandwich etc.

In which the fat and sugar are beaten together, more fat and eggs give good keeping qualities.

Whisked—swiss roll, sponge sandwich etc.

In which the eggs and sugar are whisked together to a thick cream. Best eaten when fresh, due to low fat content.

Melted—gingerbread, parkin, etc.

In which the fat is melted. This mixture improves in flavour during storage.

Mixing the Cakes

Beating

Thick mixture :- Use a wooden spoon, tilt the bowl slightly, rest on a folded tea towel to keep bowl in a firm position.
Thin mixture :- Use a hand or rotary whisk.

Creaming

Use a wooden spoon, break up fat, add the sugar and beat well. In cold weather when the fat is hard, warm the sugar slightly to make creaming easier.

Folding in

Use a metal spoon to cut through and through the mixture giving an occasional stir. This is a method of mixing the ingredients in the lightest possible way.
Continue until a smooth mixture is obtained.

Rubbing in

Cut the fat into small pieces, add to the flour. Using the finger tips, pick up the flour and the fat, rub together lightly, when mixture resembles fine breadcrumbs, proceed as directed in recipe

Electric mixers

Where electric mixer is available, follow the manufacturers instructions for the above processes.

Sieving

This ensures thorough mixing of all dry ingredients, removal of any lumps present in flour and introduces air into the mixture, thus making it light.

Stiff

Mixture too sticky to handle, keeps shape when dropped from a spoon. Plainer cakes and puddings are usually mixed to this consistency.

Soft

Mixture should readily drop from spoon when shaken, but is much too thick to pour. Rich cakes, Victoria sandwich and other creamed mixtures are usually mixed to this consistency.

Pouring

A batter-like consistency, obtained when making swiss rolls and gingerbreads.

Cooking and Cooling

Press victoria sandwich and sponge cake lightly with finger tips. If cooked the mixture feels springy, looks risen and brown. Larger cakes shrink slightly from the edge of the tin. Large cakes should be tested by placing a warm skewer in the centre, which will be quite clean when withdrawn if cooking is complete.

Cooling small cakes

Remove from oven, leave for a few minutes. Remove from tin and place on a cooling rack.

Cooling large cakes

Remove from oven, leave in tin until cool. Remove from tin carefully and place on a cooling rack. Remove paper, make sure cake is quite cold before storing in a cake tin.

Queen Cakes

Method
1 Cream the margarine and sugar.
2 Add the beaten egg, sieve flour with salt and fold in until mixed.
3 Add milk to give a soft dropping consistency.
4 Place in greaseproof cake cases, bake.

Ingredients
50g (2oz) margarine
50g (2oz) caster sugar
1 egg
75g (3oz) self raising flour
salt
milk as required

Cooking
Main oven temperature:
200–210°C
Time: 14–18 mins
Tin: baking tray
Shelf: middle
[Second oven
temperature: 190–200°C
Fan oven
temperature: 180°C]

Makes 10

Victoria Sandwich

Method
1 Grease and line tins.
2 Cream margarine with sugar until light and fluffy.
3 Gradually add lightly beaten eggs. Add a little at a time, beating well between each adddition.
4 Sieve flour and salt.
5 Fold flour into creamed mixture, stir gently until a smooth consistency is obtained.
6 Divide mixture and place in prepared tins. Bake.
7 When cooked, cool, spread with jam and sandwich together.

Ingredients
100g (4oz) margarine
100g (4oz) caster sugar
2 eggs
100g (4oz) self raising flour
pinch salt
raspberry jam

Cooking
Main oven temperature: 190°C
Time: 18–25 mins
Tin: 2 18cm (7in.)
victoria sandwich tins
Shelf: middle
[Second oven
temperature: 160–170°C
Fan oven
temperature: 170°C]

Variations on queen cake recipe and victoria sandwich recipe

Chocolate and coconut: 25g (1oz) cocoa (subtract 25g (1oz) flour), 40g (1½oz) dessicated coconut, vanilla essence, 3 5ml (tea) spoon milk.

Coffee and walnut: 3 5ml (tea) spoon instant coffee dissolved in a little warm water, 50g (2oz) walnuts, chopped.

Mixed fruit: 100g (4oz) sultanas, 50g (2oz) currants, 25g (1oz) mixed peel, 1 5ml (tea) spoon mixed spice.

Fillings for victoria sandwich, use quarter butter icing recipe (page 102).
Toppings use half glacé icing recipe (page 102).

Christmas Cake

Method

1 Line the tin with double greaseproof paper.

2 Cream fat, sugar and grated rinds until light and fluffy; beat in eggs, one at a time.

3 Add dry ingredients to mixture; combine thoroughly.

4 Mix in liquid; add extra liquid if required to form a medium dropping consistency.

5 Turn into lined tin; ensure that there are no pockets of air and the surface is flat.

6 Tie a double band of brown paper around tin so that it is approximately 7.5cm (3in.) above top of tin.

7 Place in oven slightly below middle.

8 When the cake is cooked, leave to cool in the tin. When cold turn out and carefully remove greaseproof paper.

Note: To store: wrap in fresh greaseproof paper and then completely in foil.

To allow cake to mature, make at least two months in advance.

If desired, a small amount of brandy or sherry can be brushed over the top and sides of the cake at regular intervals during storage.

Tin sizes	15cm (6in.) square 18cm (7in.) round	20cm (8in.) square 23cm (9in.) round	25cm (10in.) square 28cm (11in.) round	30cm (12in.) square 33cm (13in.) round
Ingredients				
sugar–$\frac{1}{2}$ caster, $\frac{1}{2}$ soft brown	140g (5$\frac{1}{2}$oz)	200g (8oz)	300g (12oz)	550g (22oz)
butter or margarine	140g (5$\frac{1}{2}$oz)	200g (8oz)	300g (12oz)	550g (22oz)
rind, grated	$\frac{1}{2}$ lemon and $\frac{1}{2}$ orange	$\frac{3}{4}$ lemon and $\frac{3}{4}$ orange	1 lemon and 1 orange	1$\frac{1}{4}$ lemon and 1$\frac{1}{4}$orange
eggs	3	4	6	12
plain flour	150g (6oz)	250g (10oz)	375g (15oz)	600g (24oz)
mixed spice	$\frac{1}{2}$ 5ml (tea) spoon	1 5ml (tea) spoon	2 5ml (tea) spoon	2$\frac{1}{2}$ 5ml (tea) spoon
nutmeg	$\frac{1}{4}$ 5ml (tea) spoon	$\frac{1}{2}$ 5ml (tea) spoon	$\frac{3}{4}$ 5ml (tea) spoon	1 5ml (tea) spoon
salt	$\frac{1}{4}$ 5ml (tea) spoon	$\frac{1}{2}$ 5ml (tea) spoon	$\frac{3}{4}$ 5ml (tea) spoon	1 5ml (tea) spoon
sultanas	150g (6oz)	200g (8oz)	300g (12oz)	600g (24oz)
raisins	150g (6oz)	200g (8oz)	300g (12oz)	600g (24oz)
currants	200g (8oz)	250g (10oz)	400g (16oz)	800g (32oz)
cut cherries	75g (3oz)	100g (4oz)	150g (6oz)	300g (12oz)
peel	75g (3oz)	100g (4oz)	150g (6oz)	300g (12oz)
almonds, ground	25g (1oz)	50g (2oz)	75g (3oz)	100g (4oz)
almonds, chopped	20g ($\frac{3}{4}$oz)	25g (1oz)	50g (2oz)	100g (4oz)
beer, ale, milk,	1–2 15ml (table) spoon	2–3 15ml (table) spoon	3–4 15ml (table) spoon	4–5 15ml (table) spoon
lemon or orange juice	2–3 15ml (table) spoon	3–4 15ml (table) spoon	5–6 15ml (table) spoon	6–7 15ml (table) spoon
coffee essence	$\frac{1}{4}$ 5ml (tea) spoon	$\frac{1}{4}$ 5ml (tea) spoon	$\frac{1}{2}$ 5ml (tea) spoon	$\frac{1}{2}$ 5ml (tea) spoon
almond essence	few drops	few drops	few drops	few drops
vanilla essence	few drops	few drops	few drops	few drops
rum essence	few drops	few drops	few drops	few drops
gravy browning (opt.)	few drops	few drops	few drops	few drops
cooking time	3 hours	3–3$\frac{1}{2}$ hours	3$\frac{1}{2}$–4 hours	4–4$\frac{1}{2}$ hours
main oven **temperature**	150°C (second/fan oven 130–140°C)	150°C (fan oven 130–140°C)	150°C (fan oven 130–140°C)	150°C (fan oven 130–140°C)

Swiss Roll

Method

1 Grease and line tin.
2 Whisk eggs and sugar together for 10 minutes or until mixture is thick and creamy.
3 Sieve flour and salt together, sieve half quantity of flour onto whisked mixture, fold in gently.
4 Add warm water and stir in. Sieve in remaining flour and fold in as before. Continue to stir until smooth consistency is obtained.
5 Pour into prepared tin. Bake.

Place a piece of greaseproof paper over a damp cloth. Just before removing swiss roll from oven, sprinkle paper with caster sugar. Remove swiss roll from oven, turn onto sugared paper. Remove lining paper, spread swiss roll with warm jam. Roll carefully and leave to cool on a cake rack.

Ingredients

2 eggs
50g (2oz) caster sugar
50g (2oz) plain flour
pinch salt
1 15ml (table) spoon warm water
jam

Cooking

Main oven temperature: 200°C
Time: 10–14 mins
Tin: 18 × 30cm
(7½ × 11½in.) swiss roll tin
Shelf: middle
Second oven temperature: 180–190°C
Fan oven temperature: 180–190°C

Sponge Sandwich

Method

1 Grease and line tins.
2 Whisk eggs and sugar together for 10 minutes or until mixture is thick and creamy.
3 Sieve flour and salt together, sieve half quantity of flour into thickened mixture. Fold in gently.
4 Add warm water and stir in. Sieve in remaining flour and fold in as before. Continue to stir until a smooth consistency is obtained.
5 Pour into prepared tins. Bake.
6 Remove from tins and cool. When quite cold, sandwich together with butter icing (page 102).

Ingredients

3 eggs
75g (3oz) caster sugar
75g (3oz) plain flour
pinch salt
1 15ml (table) spoon warm water
butter icing

Cooking

Main oven temperature: 200°C
Time: 18–20 mins
Tins: 2 18cm (7in.) sandwich tins
Shelf: middle
Second oven temperature: 180–190°C
Fan oven temperature: 180–190°C

Variations for sponge sandwich and swiss roll

1 Chocolate: substitute 15g (½oz) flour with 15g (½oz) cocoa.
2 Coffee: Add 1½ 5ml (tea) spoon instant coffee dissolved in a very little water. Add liquid to mixture instead of warm water (point 4).

Date and Walnut Cake

Method

1 Grease and line tin.
2 Sieve flour and salt, rub fat into flour.
3 Add sugar, dates and walnuts.
4 Beat in eggs, milk and vanilla essence.
5 Place in prepared tin. Bake.

Ingredients

200g (8oz) self raising flour
pinch salt
100g (4oz) margarine
100g (4oz) soft brown sugar
200g (8oz) stoned dates, chopped
50g (2oz) shelled walnuts, chopped
2 eggs
125ml ($\frac{1}{4}$pt) milk
a few drops of vanilla essence

Cooking

Main oven temperature: 160°C
Time: 1$\frac{1}{2}$–1$\frac{3}{4}$ hrs
Tin: 600g (1$\frac{1}{2}$lb) loaf tin
Shelf: middle
Second oven
temperature: 140–150°C
Fan oven
temperature: 130–140°C

Chocolate Cake

Method

1 Grease and line tins.
2 Cream butter, sugar and honey until light and fluffy.
3 Gradually add lightly beaten eggs. Add a little at a time, beating well between each addition.
4 Sieve flour, salt and cocoa together, fold into creamed mixture, add liquid coffee.
5 Add vanilla essence and stir well, place in prepared tins. Bake.
6 Cool cake, trim sides if it is square, spread icing over the top, fork up, cut into 16 squares. If the cake is round, fill the centre and spread the remaining icing on top and down the sides.

For icing recipe see page 104.

Ingredients

150g (6oz) butter
75g (3oz) demerara sugar
75g (3oz) liquid honey
3 eggs
115g (4$\frac{1}{2}$oz) self raising flour
pinch salt
40g (1$\frac{1}{2}$oz) cocoa
1 5ml (tea) spoon instant coffee, dissolved in hot water
vanilla essence

Cooking

Main oven temperature: 190°C
Time: 25–35 mins
Tin: 2 18cm (7in.) sandwich tins or
1 23 × 23cm (9 × 9in.) tin
Shelf: top and middle
Second oven
temperature: 170–180°C
Fan oven
temperature: 170°C

Makes 16

Streusel Cake

Method

1 Grease and line tin.
2 Cream fat and sugar until light and fluffy, add egg, beat in well.
3 Sieve flour and salt together and fold into creamed mixture, add milk to produce a soft mixture.
4 To make topping, cream the sugar and fat and combine flour, cinnamon and walnuts.
5 Spread half the cake mixture into the prepared tin, sprinkle half the topping over it.
6 Cover with remaining mixture and sprinkle the rest of the topping over the top.
7 Bake. Serve warm or cool, cut into squares.

Ingredients

75g (3oz) margarine
150g (6oz) caster sugar
1 egg
150g (6oz) self raising flour
pinch salt
125 ml ($\frac{1}{4}$pt) milk

Topping

75g (3oz) soft brown sugar
25g (1oz) margarine, melted
25g (1oz) self raising flour
1 5ml (tea) spoon cinnamon
50g (2oz) walnuts, chopped

Variation

Apple and almond : 25g (1oz) ground almonds, 1 apple, 1 5ml (tea) spoon almond essence, 75g (3oz) soft brown sugar, 25g (1oz) self raising flour, 25g (1oz) margarine. Spread all mixture in centre of cake as a filling, before cooking.

Cooking

Main oven temperature: 180°C
Time: 35–40 mins
Tin: 18 × 28 × 2·5cm
(7 × 11 × 1in.) approx.
Shelf: middle
[Second oven
  temperature: 170–180°C
  Fan oven
  temperature: 170°C]

Makes 16

Bakewell Tart

Method

1 Make up pastry (page 127). Roll out and line sandwich tin. Spread base with jam.
2 Cream margarine and sugar until light and fluffy.
3 Gradually add lightly beaten egg. Add a little at a time, beat well between each addition.
4 Beat in essences.
5 Fold in ground almonds and cake crumbs, stir well. Cover jam with this mixture.
6 Roll out pastry scraps and cut into thin strips. Arrange on top, in a lattice design. Bake.

Ingredients

150g (6oz) sweet flan pastry
(page 127)
jam
50g (2oz) margarine
50g (2oz) caster sugar
1 egg
$\frac{1}{4}$ 5ml (tea) spoon vanilla essence
$\frac{1}{2}$ 5ml (tea) spoon almond essence
25g (1oz) ground almonds
40g (1$\frac{1}{2}$oz) cake crumbs

Cooking

Main oven temperature: 190°C
Time: 35–40 mins
Tin: 18cm (7in.)
sandwich tin
Shelf: middle
[Second oven
  temperature: 170–180°C
  Fan oven
  temperature: 170°C]

Serves 4–6

Glacé Fruit Cake

Method

1 Grease and line tin.
2 Cream butter and sugar until light and fluffy, add almond essence.
3 Beat in eggs, one at a time.
4 Fold in flour, salt, ground almonds and fruits, stir in brandy.
5 Place in prepared tin, bake.

Ingredients *

200g (8oz) butter
200g (8oz) caster sugar
½ 5ml (tea) spoon almond essence
3 eggs
200g (8oz) plain flour
pinch salt
100g (4oz) ground almonds
100g (4oz) glacé cherries, chopped
50g (2oz) mixed peel
150g (6oz) crystallized pineapple, chopped
25g (1oz) crystallized ginger, chopped
50g (2oz) angelica, chopped
1 5ml (tea) spoon brandy

Cooking

Main oven temperature: 150°C
Time: 3–3½ hrs
Tin: 23cm (9in.) round cake tin
Shelf: middle
Second oven temperature: 130–140°C
Fan oven temperature: 120–130°C

Madeira Cake

Method

1 Grease and line tin.
2 Cream fat and sugar until light and fluffy.
3 Gradually add lightly beaten eggs, beating well between each addition.
Sieve flour, salt and baking powder together.
5 Fold flour and grated lemon rind into creamed mixture, add milk if necessary to obtain a smooth stiff dropping consistency.
6 Place in prepared tin. Bake.

Ingredients

100g (4oz) butter
100g (4oz) sugar
2 eggs
150g (6oz) plain flour
pinch salt
1 5ml (tea) spoon baking powder
rind of 1 lemon, grated
milk to mix

Cooking

Main oven temperature: 180°C
Time: 1–1¼ hrs
Tin: 15cm (6in.) round cake tin
Shelf: middle
Second oven temperature: 140–150°C
Fan oven temperature: 140–150°C

Variations

1 Chocolate polka dot cake: Replace caster sugar with demerara sugar. Omit the lemon rind and add 100g (4oz) chocolate polka dots.
2 Cherry cake: Omit the lemon rind, add 100g (4oz) glacé cherries, chopped and a few drops of vanilla and almond essence.
3 Coconut cake: Omit lemon rind, add 75g (3oz) coconut and a few drops vanilla essence.

Éclairs

Method

1 Put the choux pastry into a piping bag with a plain round pipe of 12mm ($\frac{1}{2}$in.).
2 Pipe into fingers approximately 10cm ($3\frac{1}{2}$–4in.) onto greased baking tray, keeping the lengths even and cut the pastry using a knife against the edge of the pipe.
3 Bake, until well risen, crisp and golden brown colour.
4 Remove from tray, slit sides with sharp, pointed knife to allow the steam to escape and place on a cake rack until cold.
5 When the éclairs are cold, fill with the whipped cream or flavoured custard.
6 Dip the top of each éclair in the glacé icing or melted chocolate.

Variations
Profiteroles*

Pipe small balls of the pastry, about the size of a walnut, using 12mm ($\frac{1}{2}$in.) plain pipe. Bake until crisp. Make a hole in the side of each profiterole—leave to cool.
Pipe whipped cream in centre through the hole. Serve coated with chocolate sauce (page 33).

Meringues

Method

1 Grease baking tray.
2 Whisk egg whites until stiff.
3 Add half sugar and continue beating.
4 Fold in remaining sugar.
5 Place spoonfuls or pipe onto baking tray. Bake until dried out.
6 When cold, sandwich together with double cream.
  See illustration opposite page 113.

Ingredients

choux pastry with 65g ($2\frac{1}{2}$oz) flour (page 127)

Fillings

1 double cream, whipped
2 flavoured custard

Toppings

1 chocolate or coffee glacé icing (100g (4oz) icing sugar) (page 102)
2 50g (2oz) chocolate, melted

Ingredients

2 egg whites
100g (4oz) caster sugar
double cream, whipped

Cooking

Main oven temperature: 200°C
Time: 35–40 mins
Tin: baking trays
Shelf: top and middle
[Second oven temperature: 180–190°C
Fan oven temperature: 190°C]

Cooking

Main oven temperature: 180°C
Time: 15–20 mins
Tin: baking trays
Shelf: top/middle
[Second oven temperature: 170–180°C
Fan oven temperature: 170–180°C]

Makes approximately 12 éclairs, 24 profiteroles

Cooking

Main oven temperature: 100°C
Time: $2\frac{1}{2}$–3 hrs
Tin: baking tray
Shelf: middle
[Second oven temperature: 90–100°C
Fan oven temperature: 90–100°C]

Makes 8–12

Gingerbread

Method

1 Grease and line tin.
2 Melt the sugar, butter and treacle in a saucepan over a gentle heat. Allow to cool. Make a well in the dry ingredients, beat in mixture.
3 Add the egg and milk.
4 Beat thoroughly to a dropping consistency and pour in prepared tin. Bake.

Variations

Add 50g (2oz) chopped crystalized ginger or pineapple to the mixture. Also 50g (2oz) flaked almonds, 25g (1oz) in mixture, and 25g (1oz) on top. When cool brush with apricot glaze.

Ingredients

200g (8oz) brown sugar
150g (6oz) butter
300g (12oz) treacle or syrup
400g (1lb) plain flour
1 5ml (tea) spoon salt
1 15ml (table) spoon ground ginger
1 10ml (dessert) spoon baking powder
1 egg
250ml ($\frac{1}{2}$pt) milk

Cooking

Main oven temperature: 160°C
Time: $1\frac{1}{4}$–$1\frac{1}{2}$ hrs
Tins: 2 23 × 13cm
(9 × 5in.) loaf tins
Shelf: middle

Second oven temperature: 140–150°C
Fan oven temperature: 140–150°C

Yorkshire Parkin

Method

1 Grease and line tin.
2 Mix all dry ingredients together.
3 Place treacle, syrup and butter in a saucepan and warm.
4 Dissolve the bicarbonate of soda in slightly warmed milk.
5 Mix all the ingredients together, pouring the liquids into the flour, stir well.
6 Pour into prepared tin and bake. Cut into squares when cold. See illustration opposite page 113.

Ingredients

100g (4oz) plain flour
200g (8oz) medium oatmeal
25g (1oz) sugar
pinch ground ginger
pinch of salt
125g (5oz) treacle
100g (4oz) golden syrup
100g (4oz) butter
$\frac{1}{2}$ 5ml (tea) spoon bicarbonate of soda
2 15ml (table) spoon milk

Cooking

Main oven temperature: 160°C
Time: 55–65 mins
Tin: 20cm (8in.)
square
Shelf: middle

Second oven temperature: 140–150°C
Fan oven temperature: 150°C

Makes 16

Rich Fruit Cake

Method

1 Grease and line tin.
2 Cream fat and sugar until light and fluffy, add eggs one at a time, beating well between each addition.
3 Sieve flour, salt and baking powder together, slowly fold into creamed mixture.
4 Add all fruit, mix well. Place mixture into prepared tin. Bake.

Ingredients*

225g (9oz) margarine or butter
225g (9oz) caster sugar
6 eggs
300g (12oz) plain flour
1½ 5ml (tea) spoon baking powder
pinch of salt
150g (6oz) sultanas
150g (6oz) currants
115g (4½oz) glacé cherries, chopped
115g (4½oz) mixed peel

Cooking

Main oven temperature: 160°C
Time: 2¼–2½ hrs
Tin: 23cm (9in.) round cake tin
Shelf: middle
[Second oven temperature: 130–140°C
Fan oven temperature: 130–140°C]

Scones

Method

1 Sieve flour, salt, and baking powder together, rub in margarine.
2 Stir in sugar.
3 Add liquid and work mixture into a soft dough.
4 Roll out to 12mm (½in.) thick. Using a 5cm (2in.) cutter, cut into small scones (approximately 14). Place on baking tray. Bake.

Variations

1 Cheese scones: ½ level 5ml (tea) spoon salt, pepper and dry mustard added to flour. 100g (4oz) finely grated cheese added to rubbed in mixture. Leave out sugar from basic recipe.
2 Date and walnut: 50g (2oz) coarsely chopped dates and 50g (2oz) chopped walnuts added to rubbed mixture.
3 Rich tea: Add 2 15ml (table) spoon caster sugar more, an egg in place of equal quantity of liquid, and 50g (2oz) dried fruit.
4 Scone round: Half quantity basic scone mix. Variations can be used, ingredients should also be halved. Roll scone mix into a round approximately 18cm (7in.) diameter. Score into 8 pieces, place on baking tray, bake.

See illustration opposite page 113.

Ingredients

300g (12oz) self raising flour
pinch salt
1 level 5ml (tea) spoon baking powder
75g (3oz) margarine
25g (1oz) caster sugar
125ml (¼pt) milk or milk and water mixed

Cooking

Main oven temperature: 240°C
Time: 8–10 mins
Tin: baking trays
Shelf: top/middle
[Second oven temperature: 220–230°C
Fan oven temperature: 210–220°C]

Cooking Scone Round

Main oven temperature: 200°C
Time: 20–30 mins
Tin: baking tray
Shelf: middle
[Second oven temperature: 190–200°C
Fan oven temperature: 190°C]

Makes 12–16

Biscuits

There is a varied range of commercially made biscuits available, but in this section we have included some which are quick and easy and can be made in batches for families, where there could be a greater demand for biscuits. Also included are recipes for those delicious florentines and flap jacks which are more costly to buy.

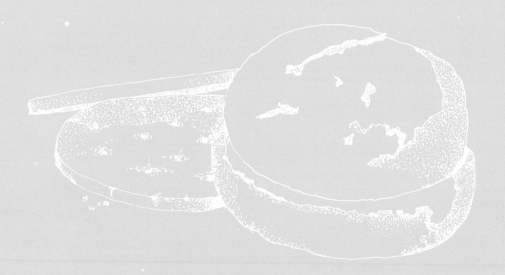

Shrewsbury Biscuits

Method

1 Cream butter and sugar, add beaten egg.
2 Stir in flour and lemon, form a firm dough.
3 Knead and roll out to 3–6mm ($\frac{1}{8}$–$\frac{1}{4}$in.) thick.
4 Cut out with a 5cm (2in.) fluted cutter, put on trays, prick over with a fork.
5 Bake until very lightly brown.

Ingredients

100g (4oz) butter
100g (4oz) caster sugar
1 egg, beaten
200g (8oz) plain flour
2 5ml (tea) spoon lemon rind, grated

Cooking

Main oven temperature: 180°C
Time: 15–20 mins
Tin: baking trays
Shelf: top and middle

Second oven
temperature: 160–170°C
Fan oven
temperature: 160°C

Makes approximately 24

Viennese Whirls

Method

1 Cream fat and sugar together until light and fluffy.
2 Sieve flour and salt, add to mixture gradually. Beat well after each addition until the mixture is smooth.
3 Using a 2.5cm (1in.) star pipe, pipe stars approximately 3cm (1$\frac{1}{4}$in.) diameter and no more than 6mm ($\frac{1}{8}$in.) high onto a tray.
4 Bake. When cooked dust with icing sugar.

Ingredients

75g (3oz) butter
25g (1oz) icing sugar
75g (3oz) plain flour
pinch salt

Cooking

Main oven temperature:
210–220°C
Time: 8–10 mins
Tin: baking trays
Shelf: top and middle

Second oven
temperature: 190–200°C
Fan oven
temperature: 190–200°C

Makes 20

Coconut Drops

Method

1 Gradually beat the coconut into the sweetened condensed milk. Mix well.
2 Form into balls, place on baking tray, decorate with cherries or pineapple and angelica leaves. Bake.

Ingredients

200g (8oz) dessicated coconut
125ml ($\frac{1}{4}$pt) sweetened condensed milk
7 glacé cherries or
25g (1oz) crystallized pineapple angelica

Cooking

Main oven temperature: 200°C
Time: 10–15 mins
Tin: baking trays
Shelf: top and middle

Second oven
temperature: 180–190°C
Fan oven
temperature: 180–190°C

Makes 28

Almond Shorties

Method

1 Sift flour into a mixing bowl with icing sugar, salt and softened butter.
2 Knead together into a soft dough.
3 Roll out thinly, cut out 24 rounds using a 5cm (2in.) fluted cutter. Place on a baking tray, prick with a fork.
4 Whisk egg whites until fairly stiff, fold in ground almonds, caster sugar, almond essence and lemon juice.
5 Using a 20mm ($\frac{3}{4}$in.) star pipe, pipe mixture onto the biscuits, leaving 12mm ($\frac{1}{2}$in.) space around the edge.
6 Sprinkle a few flaked almonds on top and place a piece glacé cherry in the centre. Bake.

Ingredients

150g (6oz) plain flour
75g (3oz) icing sugar
$\frac{1}{4}$ 5ml (tea) spoon salt
100g (4oz) butter, softened

Topping

2 egg whites
100g (4oz) ground almonds
75g (3oz) caster sugar
a few drops almond essence
$\frac{1}{2}$ 5ml (tea) spoon lemon juice

Decoration

10g ($\frac{1}{3}$oz) almonds, flaked
3 glacé cherries

Cooking

Main oven temperature: 180°C
Time: 15–20 mins
Tin: baking trays
Shelf: top and middle

Second oven
temperature: 160–170°C
Fan oven
temperature: 160–170°C

Makes 24

Nut Cookies

Method

1 Cream butter and sugar until light and fluffy, add flour and salt, form into a dough.
2 Place on a floured board, shape into a 25cm (10in.) roll.
3 Cut a piece of foil approximately 15 × 45cm (6 × 18in.), sprinkle with finely chopped almonds.
4 Roll dough in almonds to coat the sides, wrap in foil and place in refrigerator to firm up.
5 Cut roll into 6mm ($\frac{1}{4}$in.) slices, place slightly apart on baking trays. Bake.

Ingredients *

150g (6oz) butter
100g (4oz) soft light brown sugar
200g (8oz) plain flour
$\frac{1}{4}$ 5ml (tea) spoon salt
50g (2oz) almonds, finely chopped

Cooking

Main oven temperature: 160°C
Time: 15–20 mins
Tin: baking trays
Shelf: top and middle

Second oven
temperature: 150–160°C
Fan oven
temperature: 150°C

Makes approximately 40

Florentines

Method

1 Line the base of each patty tin section with a small disc of rice paper.
2 Place cherries, peel and almonds in a saucepan; add butter, sugar, honey and cream, and warm over a gentle heat until mixed together.
3 Place half 5ml (tea) spoon of the mixture into lined patty tins and spread evenly.
4 Bake until golden brown.
5 Cool slightly, remove from tins and allow to cool.
6 Coat the bases with melted chocolate. When nearly set make fork mark ripples and leave to set.

Ingredients*

15g (½oz) glacé cherries, finely chopped
40g (1½oz) mixed peel, finely chopped
100g (4oz) almonds, blanched and finely chopped
50g (2oz) butter
50g (2oz) caster sugar
15g (½oz) honey
1 15ml (table) spoon cream
100g (4oz) plain chocolate

Cooking

Main oven temperature: 180°C
Time: 6–8 mins
Tin: 12 section patty tins
Shelf: top and middle
Second oven temperature: 170–180°C
Fan oven temperature: 170°C

Makes approximately 50

Easter Biscuits

Method

1 Cream butter and sugar and beat in egg yolk.
2 Fold sieved flour, salt and fruit into creamed mixture. Add spice, essence and enough milk to make a soft dough.
3 Place in a refrigerator to become firm.
4 Knead lightly and roll out 6mm (¼in.) thick. Cut out with a 5cm (2in.) cutter.
5 Put on a baking tray; prick over with a fork.
6 Bake for 10 minutes and then brush the biscuits with egg white and sprinkle with sugar. Bake for a further 5–10 minutes.

Ingredients

75g (3oz) butter or margarine
65g (2½oz) caster sugar
1 egg, separated
150g (6oz) self raising flour
pinch of salt
50g (2oz) currants
15g (½oz) mixed peel
2 drops of brandy essence
½ 5ml (tea) spoon mixed spice
2 15ml (table) spoon milk
a little sugar

Cooking

Main oven temperature: 200°C
Time: 15–20 mins
Tin: baking trays
Shelf: top and middle
Second oven temperature: 180–190°C
Fan oven temperature: 180°C

Makes approximately 24

Shortbread

Method

1 Sieve flour, ground rice and salt into a mixing bowl.
2 Add the sugar; work in the butter gradually, kneading by hand.
3 When a soft pliable dough is formed turn on to a floured board and knead until smooth and free from cracks.
4 Press into the tin and smooth with a palette knife.
5 Crimp the edges with a fork and mark into 6.
6 When cooked dredge with caster sugar and cut into wedges when cold.

Ingredients

125g (5oz) plain flour
25g (1oz) ground rice
pince of salt
50g (2oz) caster sugar
100g (4oz) butter

Variations

1 Sultana and walnut:
   25g (1oz) sultanas, chopped
   25g (1oz) walnuts, chopped

2 Almond and cherry:
   25g (1oz) cherries, chopped
   few drops almond essence

Cooking

Main oven temperature: 150°C
Time: 45–65 mins
Tin: 18cm (7in.) round sandwich tin
Shelf: middle

Second oven temperature: 140–150°C
Fan oven temperature: 130–140°C

Makes 6

Flapjacks

Method

1 Melt fat, sugar and syrup together in a saucepan.
2 Add oats and salt and mix well together.
3 Put into a greased tin; bake.
4 While still warm cut into fingers.

Variations

1 150g (6oz) corn flakes crushed instead of 200g (8oz) oats
2 50g (2oz) coconut instead of 50g (2oz) oats

Ingredients

100g (4oz) butter
25g (1oz) dark brown sugar
2 15ml (table) spoon golden syrup
200g (8oz) rolled oats
pinch of salt

Cooking

Main oven temperature: 190°C
Time: 25–30 mins
Tin: 23 × 23cm (9 × 9in.) tin
Shelf: top

Second oven temperature: 180°C
Fan oven temperature: 170–180°C

Makes approximately 24

Macaroons

Method
1 Line baking trays with rice paper.
2 Whisk egg white until stiff, add ground almonds and caster sugar and essences. Beat well.
3 Using a 12mm ($\frac{1}{2}$in.) pipe, pipe onto the baking trays or place small spoonfuls of mixture onto baking trays. Place an almond on top of each, brush with egg white, bake until pale golden brown.

Ingredients
1 large egg white or 1$\frac{1}{2}$ standard egg whites
50g (2oz) ground almonds
75g (3oz) caster sugar
few drops almond essence
few drops vanilla essence
almonds, split
egg white to brush

Cooking
Main oven temperature: 180°C
Time: 20–25 mins
Tin: 2 baking trays
Shelf: top and middle

Second oven temperature: 160–170°C
Fan oven temperature: 160–170°C

Makes 10–12

Cheese Biscuits

Method
1 Sieve flour, salt, mustard and pepper together.
2 Rub fat into flour. Add cheese.
3 Add sufficient beaten egg to form a pliable dough.
4 Roll out pastry 3mm ($\frac{1}{8}$in.) and using a 5cm (2in.) cutter, shape biscuits.
5 Arrange on a baking tray, prick well, glaze with egg, bake.
6 Serve as they are, with cheese or pipe cream cheese on top and decorate with pineapple, tomato or sprinkle with paprika pepper.

Variations
Cheese Straws
Make up mixture as above. Roll out cheese pastry 3mm ($\frac{1}{8}$in.) thick and cut into thin strips about 8cm (3in.) long. Arrange pastry strips on baking tray. Bake.
Serve on their own or with a cheese dip.

Ingredients
150g (6oz) plain flour
pinch salt and pepper
$\frac{1}{4}$ 5ml (tea) spoon dry mustard
100g (4oz) margarine
100g (4oz) strong cheese, finely grated
egg, beaten, to bind and glaze

Cooking
Main oven temperature: 200°C
Time: 10–12 mins
Tin: baking trays
Shelf: top and middle

Second oven temperature: 180–190°C
Fan oven temperature: 180–190°C

Makes approximately 24

Pastry

In this section there are the recipes for making different kinds of pastry. Their use is described in appropriate recipes given throughout the book.

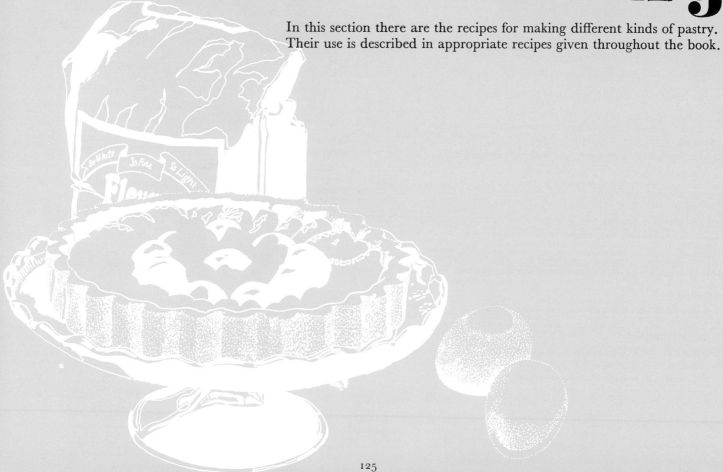

Short Crust Pastry

Method

1 Sieve flour and salt into mixing bowl.
2 Rub in fat.
3 Mix to a stiff dough, using cold water. Turn out onto a floured board and knead lightly. Use as required.

Ingredients

400g (1lb) plain flour
pinch salt
100g (4oz) lard
100g (4oz) margarine
cold water to mix

Suet Crust Pastry

Method

1 Mix flour, baking powder, suet and salt together.
2 Mix to a soft dough using cold water.
3 Turn out onto a floured board and knead lightly. Use as required.

Ingredients

400g (1lb) plain flour
2 5ml (tea) spoon baking powder
150g (6oz) suet, chopped or shredded
2 5ml (tea) spoon salt
cold water to mix

Hot Water Crust Pastry

Method

1 Sieve flour and salt into a warm mixing bowl.
2 Melt lard in a small saucepan with milk and water and bring to the boil.
3 Pour into the centre of the flour and mix quickly into a paste.
4 Turn out on to a floured board and knead lightly. Use as required. Do not allow mixture to cool.

Ingredients

300g (12oz) plain flour
1½ 5ml (tea) spoon salt
75g (3oz) lard
125ml (¼pt) milk and water

Flan Pastry

Method

1 Sieve flour, and salt together. Make a well in the centre, drop in egg and margarine.
2 Knead mixture together until a soft pliable dough is formed. Use as required.

Ingredients

300g (12oz) plain flour
pinch of salt
1 egg
200g (8oz) margarine

Variations

Sweet flan pastry

50g (2oz) caster sugar

Savoury flan pastry

100g (4oz) margarine, replace by
100g (4oz) cream cheese

Choux Pastry

Method

1 Place butter and water in a saucepan and bring to the boil.
2 Remove from the heat, add the flour, beat well.
3 Cook until paste comes away from the sides.
4 Leave to cool, add eggs gradually, beating continuously.
5 The mixture should be a soft piping consistency which will hold its shape. Use as required.

Ingredients

40g (1½oz) butter
125ml (¼pt) water
65g (2½oz) plain flour
2 eggs, beaten

Cheese Pastry

Method

1 Sieve flour, pepper and salt into a mixing bowl.
2 Rub in fat and add cheese.
3 Add water to make a stiff dough. Turn onto a floured board and knead lightly. Use as required.

Ingredients

400g (1lb) plain flour
½ 5ml (tea) spoon salt and pepper
300g (12oz) margarine
100g (4oz) cheese, grated
3–4 15ml (table) spoon cold water

Rough Puff Pastry

Method

1 Sieve flour and salt into mixing bowl.
2 Cut fat into small pieces, add to the flour.
3 Mix to stiff dough using lemon juice and cold water. Turn onto a floured board and roll to form an oblong.
4 Fold in three, bringing the top third over the centre and folding the bottom up over both layers.
5 Half turn the pastry and roll to an oblong again.
6 Repeat this process three to four times.
7 Roll out as required.

Note: The pastry is improved if it is allowed to rest for a short time in the refrigerator for a few minutes between rollings.

Ingredients

400g (1lb) plain flour
2 5ml (tea) spoon salt
300g (12oz) fat (half lard, half margarine)
squeeze of lemon juice
cold water to mix

Flaky Pastry

Method

1 Mix the fat together with a knife until it is a soft consistency. Divide into four.
2 Sieve flour and salt into a mixing bowl.
3 Rub one quarter of fat into flour.
4 Mix to an elastic dough using lemon juice and cold water.
5 Turn out onto a floured board and knead lightly.
6 Roll into an oblong, distribute one quarter of the fat in small pieces over two thirds of the pastry. Fold into three, placing the edge without fat over the centre and bring down the top third over the middle, forming alternate layers of fat and dough.
7 Half turn the pastry and roll out again repeat until all the fat has been added. Roll out and fold once more before using.

Note: The pastry is improved if it is allowed to rest for a short time wrapped in greaseproof in the refrigerator for a few minutes between rollings.

Ingredients

300g (12oz) fat (half lard, half margarine)
400g (1lb) plain flour
1 5ml (tea) spoon salt
lemon juice
cold water to mix

Yeast Cookery

Home made bread is so different in texture and flavour, compared with the shop bought variety, that you will probably find that you will want to make it more and more often and also try out the richer yeast mixtures for buns, doughnuts and rum babas.

Mixing the Dough

When making a yeast dough, keep all the utensils and ingredients warm, this helps the yeast to produce gas, thus making the dough rise. Take special care not to overheat the mixture, this will inactivate the yeast.

Kneading: Dough is kneaded to make a soft silky mixture, it also makes an even texture mixture by distributing the gases. The mixture is brought from the ouside to the centre, (using the knuckles) working into a smooth soft dough.

Proving: Leave to prove in a warm atmosphere, humid if possible.

Ingredients

Flour: Plain flour is always used when making up yeast mixtures the yeast takes the place of baking powder as a raising agent.

Yeast: All the recipes in this section have been tested using dried yeast, because this is an easy way of keeping a constant supply of yeast in the store cupboard. If fresh yeast is available use double the weight recommended for dried yeast. Cream it with the sugar and it is ready for use. Ensure that fresh yeast is not stale, it should be putty coloured. If it is tinged with brown, crumbly and has a strong smell, it is stale and may not activate.

Fruit: Wash, clean and pick over, dry. Add to mixture after the first proving.

Cooking and cooling

Testing: Lift from the tin. Tap the base, if it sounds hollow and the exterior is nicely browned, cooking is complete.

Cooling: Remove from tin, place on a cooling rack.

White Bread

Method

1 Warm water, mix sugar with a little water, sprinkle dried yeast into sweetened water, leave in warm place to activate.
2 Rub butter into warmed flour and salt.
3 Add yeast mixture and liquid to flour and mix into a dough. Leave covered to double its size in a warm place ($\frac{3}{4}$–1 hour).
4 Knead until smooth.
5 Divide into 2 pieces, shape and place into tins. Leave in warm place to prove (15–20 minutes).
6 Bake.

Variations

Dinner rolls and milk loaf: Use milk instead of water and add a beaten egg.

Wholemeal rolls: Use milk instead of water and add a beaten egg. Substitute half flour for wholemeal flour.

When making rolls, at stage 5 divide dough into 16 pieces, shape and place onto greased baking trays. Dinner rolls should be glazed with beaten egg before baking.

See illustration opposite page 128.

Ingredients

250ml ($\frac{1}{2}$pt) water approx.
1 5ml (tea) spoon sugar
7g ($\frac{1}{4}$oz) dried yeast
25g (1oz) butter
400g (1lb) flour, sieved and warmed with $\frac{1}{2}$ 5ml (tea) spoon salt

Cooking

Main oven temperature: 220°C
Time: 20–25 mins
Tin: 2 400g (1lb) loaf tins
Shelf: middle

Second oven temperature: 210–220°C
Fan oven temperature: 210°C

Cooking

Main oven temperature: 220°C
Time: milk loaf 20–25 mins; dinner rolls 15 mins
Tin: milk loaf 2 400g (1lb) loaf tins; rolls baking trays
Shelf: top and middle

Second oven temperature: 210–220°C
Fan oven temperature: 210°C

Makes 2 loaves or 16 rolls

Wholemeal Loaf

Method

1 Activate yeast with warm sugar water.
2 Rub fat into flour and salt, warm.
3 Add yeast mixture and liquid to flour, knead well, leave covered to double in size in a warm place.
4 Knead until smooth. Put in greased tin, leave to prove 20–30 minutes.
5 Bake.

Ingredients

15g ($\frac{1}{2}$oz) dried yeast
15g ($\frac{1}{2}$oz) sugar
250ml ($\frac{1}{2}$pt) warm water (approx.)
15g ($\frac{1}{2}$oz) butter
400g (1lb) wholemeal flour
$\frac{1}{2}$ level 15ml (table) spoon salt

Cooking

Main oven temperature: 220–230°C
Time: 20–30 mins
Tin: 18cm (7in.) sandwich tin
Shelf: top/middle

Second oven temperature: 210–220°C
Fan oven temperature: 210–220°C

Makes 1 large loaf

Bridge Rolls

Method

1 Heat milk, add half to sugar and sprinkle dried yeast into sweetened milk, leave in warm place to activate. Dissolve butter in rest of milk.
2 Beat eggs and add to milk.
3 Sieve flour and salt, make a well, add liquids and mix into a smooth dough. Leave covered in warm place to double in size ($\frac{3}{4}$–1 hour).
4 Knead until smooth, shape into small fingers, place close together on a well-greased baking tray, brush with egg and salt, leave to prove for 20–30 minutes.
5 Brush again and bake.

Ingredients*

125–175ml ($\frac{1}{4}$–$\frac{1}{3}$pt) milk
25g (1oz) sugar
18g ($\frac{3}{4}$oz) dried yeast
25g (1oz) butter
2 eggs
400g (1lb) flour, warmed and sieved
7g ($\frac{1}{4}$oz) salt
egg and salt to glaze

Cooking

Main oven temperature: 220°C
Time: 15–20 mins
Tin: baking trays
Shelf: top and middle
Second oven temperature: 210–220°C
Fan oven temperature: 210°C

Makes 50

Onion Bread

Method

1 Activate the dried yeast in warm sweetened liquid.
2 Sieve flour and salt together, rub in margarine, add onion soup.
3 Add liquid, yeast and egg to dry ingredients, knead into a smooth dough, adding extra liquid if necessary.
4 Cover and leave in a warm place, to double in size, 20–30 minutes.
5 Knock the dough back and knead until smooth.
6 Divide dough into two and make one into a cottage loaf and the other into a plait.
7 Place on greased baking trays, leave to prove for 20–30 minutes.
8 Glaze with beaten egg. Bake.

Variations

1 5ml (tea) spoon mixed herbs or 50g (2oz) cheese grated, may be added to the onion soup.

Ingredients

7g ($\frac{1}{4}$oz) dried yeast
7g ($\frac{1}{4}$oz) sugar
375ml ($\frac{3}{4}$pt) milk and water mixed
600g (1$\frac{1}{2}$lb) flour
15g ($\frac{1}{2}$oz) salt
15g ($\frac{1}{2}$oz) margarine
500ml (1pt) size dried onion soup
1 egg
1 egg to glaze

Cooking

Main oven temperature: 230°C
Time: 20–25 mins
Tin: baking trays
Shelf: top and middle
Second oven temperature: 210–220°C
Fan oven temperature: 210°C

Makes 2

Malt Loaf

Method

1 Activate yeast in warm sugar water.
2 Sieve flour and salt, add sultanas.
3 Warm malt, treacle and fat until melted.
4 Add liquids to dry ingredients making a soft sticky dough, adding more water if necessary.
5 Knead on a floured board until smooth, divide into 2, shape into oblongs and place in greased tins.
6 Leave to rise until the dough reaches just above the top of the tins, this could take up to 1½ hours. Bake.
7 When cooked, brush all over with sugar glaze.

Ingredients

15g (½oz) dried yeast
15g (½oz) sugar
125ml (¼pt) water approx.
400g (1lb) plain flour
1 5ml (tea) spoon salt
100g (4oz) sultanas
4 15ml (table) spoon malt
1 15ml (table) spoon treacle
25g (1oz) butter

Sugar glaze
1 5ml (tea) spoon sugar to
1 5ml (tea) spoon water, boiled together

Cooking

Main oven temperature: 200°C
Time: 25–35 mins
Tin: 2 400g (1lb) loaf tins
Shelf: middle

Second oven temperature: 180–190°C
Fan oven temperature: 190°C

Makes 2

Hot Cross Buns

Method

1 Activate yeast with sweetened milk.
2 Sieve flour and salt, rub in fat, add sugar, spices and fruit.
3 Add liquid and egg to dry ingredients using a little more milk if necessary to make a soft dough, cover and leave in a warm place to double in size.
4 Knead until smooth, divide into 12 pieces, shape into rounds, place on greased baking trays. Mark each bun with a cross cut. Leave to prove 15–20 minutes.
5 Recut crosses and bake.
6 When cooked, brush with sugar glaze.

Variation

A paste of 25g (1oz) butter, softened, 50g (2oz) flour and 4 15ml (table) spoon water may be piped to form a cross over each bun after shaping (point 4).

Ingredients

7g (¼oz) dried yeast
1 5ml (tea) spoon sugar
125ml (¼pt) milk (approx.)
300g (12oz) plain flour
1 5ml (tea) spoon salt
25g (1oz) margarine
50g (2oz) sugar
1 5ml (tea) spoon mixed spice
1 5ml (tea) spoon ground cinnamon
½ 5ml (tea) spoon ground nutmeg
100g (4oz) currants
1 egg, beaten

Sugar glaze
1 5ml (tea) spoon sugar to
1 5ml (tea) spoon water boiled together

Cooking

Main oven temperature: 220°C
Time: 15–20 mins
Tin: baking trays
Shelf: top and middle

Second oven temperature: 210–220°C
Fan oven temperature: 210°C

Makes 12

Chelsea Buns

Method
1 Activate the yeast in warm sweetened milk.
2 Sieve flour and salt, rub in margarine. Add yeast and make a soft dough. Add extra milk if necessary.
3 Knead well, cover and leave in warm place to double in size.
4 Knock back and knead well. Roll into a 25cm (10in.) square.
5 Brush with melted butter, sprinkle with sugar, currants and spice. Roll up like a swiss roll.
6 Divide into 9. Place in greased tin, leave to prove for about 20 minutes.
7 Bake. When cooked, brush with glaze.

Ingredients
7g (¼oz) dried yeast
125ml (¼pt) milk (approx.)
1 5ml (tea) spoon sugar
200g (8oz) plain flour
½ 5ml (tea) spoon salt
25g (1oz) margarine
25g (1oz) butter, melted
25–50g (1–2oz) sugar
100g (4oz) currants
½ 5ml (tea) spoon mixed spice

Sugar glaze
1 5ml (tea) spoon sugar to
1 5ml (tea) spoon water
boiled together

Cooking
Main oven temperature: 220°C
Time: 15–20 mins
Tin: 23 × 23cm
(9 × 9in.)
Shelf: middle
[Second oven
temperature: 210–220°C
Fan oven
temperature: 210°C]

Makes 9

Croissants

Method
1 Activate yeast in warm sweetened water.
2 Sieve flour and salt and add yeast, melted butter and enough milk and water to give a soft dough.
3 Knead lightly, cover and allow to rest for 30 minutes in refrigerator. Soften the butter and divide into 3.
4 Roll dough out into an oblong approximately 64 × 18cm (27 × 7in.), continue as for flaky pastry (page 128) until all fat is incorporated. Rest covered in refrigerator between each rolling.
5 Divide and cut dough into 4. Roll each piece into an oblong 46 × 23cm (15 × 9in.), and cut to produce 4–5 triangles 2 sides 23cm (9in.) and one side 15cm (6in.) for base.
6 Roll triangles up from the base to the point and curl ends round to form a crescent. Re-roll trimmings if required.
7 Place on greased tray, prove for 15–20 minutes. Brush well with egg. Bake.

Ingredients
15g (½oz) dried yeast
1 5ml (tea) spoon sugar
125ml (¼pt) warm water
500g (1lb 4oz) flour
salt
40g (1½oz) butter, melted
250ml (½pt) milk and water mixed
200g (8oz) butter
beaten egg to glaze

Cooking
Main oven temperature: 230°C
Time: 10–15 mins
Tin: baking trays
Shelf: top and middle
[Second oven
temperature: 210–220°C
Fan oven
temperature: 210–220°C]

Makes 16–20

Doughnuts

Method

1 Activate yeast in warm sweetened milk.
2 Sieve flour and salt, rub in margarine (add ingredients for variations).
3 Add liquid to flour mixture, knead until smooth.
4 Put in a warm place to double in size.
5 Knead well and divide into 12. Shape into rounds. If making the almond variation, roll the pieces of dough into a circle, put half 5ml (tea) spoon raspberry jam in the centre and draw the edges together to form a ball.
6 Place on a greased baking tray, leave to prove.
7 When proved, deep fat fry in hot fat at 180°C, turning once.
8 Toss cooked doughnuts in sugar coating.

Ingredients

7g ($\frac{1}{4}$oz) dried yeast
65ml ($\frac{1}{8}$pt) warm milk
1 5ml (tea) spoon sugar
200g (8oz) plain flour
$\frac{1}{4}$ 5ml (tea) spoon salt
50g (2oz) margarine
egg and water (to make 65ml ($\frac{1}{8}$pt))
fat or oil for frying

Coating

caster sugar

Variations
Cinnamon and apple

1 5ml (tea) spoon cinnamon
100g (4oz) eating apple, chopped coarsely

Fruity

50g (2oz) raisins
25g (1oz) sultanas
25g (1oz) mixed peel
25g (1oz) glacé cherries, chopped

Almond

50g (2oz) roasted almonds, chopped
raspberry jam (added after first proving)   Makes 12

Rum Babas

Method

1 Activate yeast in warm sweetened water.
2 Sieve flour and salt together, add liquid and beat into a smooth batter. Allow to rise for $\frac{1}{2}$ hour.
3 Beat in egg and butter.
4 Sprinkle currants into base of greased tins.
5 Divide batter between tins. Leave to prove until the mixture rises to the top of the tins.
6 Bake.
7 Make a rum syrup by dissolving the sugar in the water and bringing the liquid to the boil and boiling for 5 minutes. Then add the rum and lemon.
8 When the babas are cooked, turn them out and soak them well in the rum syrup.
9 When cold, pipe with whipped cream.

See illustration opposite page 128.

Ingredients
Dough

7g ($\frac{1}{4}$oz) dried yeast
65ml ($\frac{1}{8}$pt) warm water
15ml (tea) spoon sugar
115g ($4\frac{1}{2}$oz) flour
pinch salt
1 egg
25g (1oz) butter, melted
currants
double cream, whipped

Syrup

150g (6oz) sugar
166ml ($\frac{1}{3}$pt) water
rum flavouring
squeeze lemon

Cooking

Main oven temperature: 220°C
Time: 15–20 mins
Tin: 6 border (ring) tins
Shelf: top

Second oven temperature: 210–220°C
Fan oven temperature: 210°C

Makes 6

Savarin

Method

1 Make as for rum babas, but put flaked almonds in the bottom of one large savarin tin and put all the mixture in together.
2 When cooked, turn out straight away, allow to cool slightly.
3 To make the syrup, dissolve the sugar in water and bring slowly to the boil, do not stir. Boil for 5 minutes. Add flavouring.
4 Soak savarin in syrup, pile fruit in centre, and pipe cream around the edge.

Ingredients
Dough

double rum baba mixture
flaked almonds

Syrup

150g (6oz) sugar
166ml ($\frac{1}{3}$pt) water
squeeze of lemon
juice from fruit
65ml ($\frac{1}{8}$pt) sherry (optional)

Decoration

flaked almonds, 1 large tin pineapple, cream

Cooking

Main oven temperature: 200°C
Time: 35–45 mins
Tin: 23cm (9in.) savarin tin
Shelf: top and middle

Second oven temperature: 190–200°C
Fan oven temperature: 190°C

Serves 8–12

Preserves

This section includes recipes for jams and marmalades, pickles and chutneys. Home preserves generally are more flavourful and nutritious than their commercial equivalents. Also, if they are made when the fresh produce is in season they are cheaper.

General Notes

1 Do not use a pan that overlaps the perimeter of the chromium trim on a radiant hotplate.
2 To allow for a full rolling boil, the pan should be no more than one third full when all the ingredients have been added.
3 Use firm fruit or vegetables.
4 Preserving sugar gives clear jam, however granulated sugar is cheaper and gives equally good flavour.
5 Crystallization may be caused if sugar is not completely dissolved before bringing jam to the boil. Over boiling will affect the flavour and darken jam.
6 To test jam for setting:
   If a jam thermometer is available, boil jam to 104°C. Marmalade should be boiled to 106°C.
   If a thermometer is not available, remove pan from heat, place sample of jam on a cold dish and cool quickly (i.e. in a freezer or frozen food storage compartment of a refrigerator). When cold, it will crinkle and hold the mark of a finger run through it, if it is ready.

Apricot Jam

Method

1 Place soaked fruit, lemon juice and liquor into a pan and cook over low heat until soft, about ½ hour.
2 Add warmed sugar, stir until dissolved.
3 Slowly bring to the boil. Boil until jam reaches setting point.
4 Add almonds when the temperature is reached.
5 Leave to cool so that the almonds do not float to the surface.
6 Fill warmed jars carefully, seal and label.

Ingredients

400g (1lb) dried apricots } soaked
1½ litre (3pt) water } overnight
juice 1 lemon
1½kg (3lb) preserving sugar, warmed
25g (1oz) almonds, blanched and shredded

Makes 2–3kg (4–6lb)

Raspberry Jam

Method

1 Wash the fruit, simmer gently over a low heat to draw out the juice for 15–20 minutes or until soft.
2 Add warmed sugar, stirring until it is dissolved.
3 Boil until jam reaches setting point.
4 Fill warmed jars, seal and label.

Ingredients

2kg (4lb) frozen or fresh raspberries, hulled
2kg (4lb) sugar

Makes 3½kg (7lb)

Plum Jam

Method

1 Wash fruit, remove stones and cut in half. Crack some stones and remove kernels.
2 Place plums, kernels, and water in a pan and simmer for ½ hour or until soft.
3 Add warmed sugar, stirring until dissolved and boil rapidly until setting point is reached.
4 Pour jam into warm jars, seal and label.

Ingredients

3kg (6lb) plums
1 litre (1¾pt) water
3kg (6lb) sugar

Makes 5kg (10lb)

Lemon Curd

Method

1 Put all ingredients into the top of a double pan or in a basin standing in a pan of simmering water.
2 Stir until sugar has dissolved, stirring from time to time until the curd thickens.
3 Fill warmed jars, seal and label.
Store in a cool place, use within 1 month.

Ingredients

6 lemons, juice and finely grated rind
6 eggs, well beaten
150g (6oz) butter
600g (1½lb) sugar

Makes 1½kg (3lb)

Mincemeat

Method

1 Mix all the ingredients together, cover and leave for two days, stirring occasionally.
2 Bottle and label. Use within 3 months.

Ingredients

50g (2oz) almonds, chopped
100g (4oz) apples, peeled and cored
300g (12oz) raisins, chopped
300g (12oz) sultanas, chopped
200g (8oz) currants, chopped
100g (4oz) mixed peel
1 carrot, peeled and chopped
200g (8oz) suet, chopped
300g (12oz) demerara sugar
125ml ($\frac{1}{4}$pt) brandy or rum
1 orange, juice and grated rind
1 lemon, juice and grated rind
5ml (tea) spoon mixed spice

Makes 2–2$\frac{1}{2}$kg (4–5lb)

Three Fruit Marmalade

Method

1 Halve fruit, extract juice and pips. If pith is thick, remove part. Shred peel to the thickness required.
2 Put peel, juice and water into pan. Tie pips in a muslin bag and place in pan and bring to the boil, then simmer gently for about 2 hours until the peel is tender.
3 Squeeze bag of pips to release any liquid and remove.
4 Stir warmed sugar in over gentle heat until sugar has dissolved.
5 Boil rapidly until marmalade is at setting point.
6 Leave 1 hour to stand, and stir.
7 Turn into warm, dry jars, seal and label.

Ingredients

2 grapefruit
4 lemons   } 1$\frac{1}{2}$kg (5lb) of fruit
2 sweet oranges
3 litres (6pt) water
3kg (6lb) preserving sugar

Makes 4–5kg (8–10lb)

Orange Marmalade

Method

1. Halve fruit, extract juice and pips. If pith thick, remove part. Shred peel to thickness required.
2. Put peel, juice and water into pan. Tie pips in a muslin bag, and place in pan and bring to the boil, then simmer gently for about 2 hours, until peel is tender.
3. Squeeze bag of pips to release any liquid, remove.
4. Stir warmed sugar in over gentle heat until sugar has dissolved.
5. Boil rapidly until marmalade is at setting point.
6. Leave 1 hour to stand, and stir.
7. Turn into warm, dry jars, seal and label.

Ingredients

8 seville oranges
3 sweet oranges
2 lemons
5 litres (9pt) water
4kg (8lb) of preserving sugar

Makes 4–6kg (9–12lb)

Red Cabbage

Method

1. Quarter cabbage, slice away the stalk, shred cabbage finely.
2. Place in a large basin and sprinkle each layer with salt. Leave for 24 hours.
3. Rinse and drain.
4. Pack cabbage loosely into bottles and cover with cold spiced vinegar.

Ready for use after one week, use within 3 months.

Ingredients

2kg (4lb) red cabbage
25g (1oz) salt

Spiced Vinegar

1 litre (2pt) malt vinegar
15g (½oz) peppercorns
7g (¼oz) allspice
15g (½oz) mustard seeds
5ml (tea) spoon mace

} place in muslin bag, add to vinegar and stand before use

Makes 2½–3kg (5–6lb)

Piccalilli

Method

1 Cut the vegetables into small pieces, sprinkle salt in layers.
2 Cover and leave for 2 hours.
3 Drain vegetables, placing in large pan, add 2 litres (4pt) of vinegar, bring to the boil.
4 Blend the turmeric, sugar, cornflour and mustard with ¼ litre (½pt) vinegar, add to vegetables.
5 Simmer gently until vegetables are just cooked and sauce thickens.
6 Pot, seal and label.

Ingredients

3kg (6lb) prepared mixed vegetables (cauliflower, cucumber, marrow, small onions)
2 15ml (table) spoon salt
15g (½oz) turmeric
175g (7oz) sugar
35g (1½oz) cornflour
85g (3½oz) dry mustard
2¼ litres (4½pt) vinegar

Makes 4½–5kg (10–12lb)

Plum Chutney

Method

1 Place all ingredients in a saucepan.
2 Bring to the boil and simmer until of the desired consistency.
3 Pot, seal and label.

Ingredients

1½kg (3lb) plums, stoned
400g (1lb) cooking apples, peeled, cored and chopped
400g (1lb) onions, chopped
400g (1lb) raisins
150g (6oz) brown sugar
1 5ml (tea) spoon ground ginger
1 5ml (tea) spoon allspice
¼ 5ml (tea) spoon each of cayenne pepper, ground cloves, mustard and nutmeg
25g (1oz) salt
500ml (1pt) vinegar

Makes approximately 3½kg (7lb)

Hot Spicy Chutney

Method

1 Place apples and onions in a saucepan with garlic, salt, brown sugar and vinegar.
2 Bring to the boil and simmer until soft. Put through a sieve or blender.
3 Stir in the raisins. Blend a little of the mixture with the ginger, mustard and cayenne pepper and add to the mixture.
4 Leave in a warm place overnight to thicken and blend.
5 Pot, seal and label.

Note: This chutney can be used as an accompaniment with curry. For a really hot chutney, the quantities for the ginger, mustard and cayenne pepper can be doubled.

Ingredients

1½kg (3lb) cooking apples, peeled, cored and chopped
400g (1lb) onions, chopped
4 cloves garlic, crushed
75g (3oz) salt
600g (1½lb) brown sugar
1 litre (2pt) vinegar
600g (1½lb) seedless raisins
50g (2oz) ground ginger
50g (2oz) dry mustard
7g (¼oz) cayenne pepper

Makes approximately 3½kg (7lb)

Apple and Date Chutney

Method

1 Place all ingredients into a saucepan. Bring to the boil and simmer until of the desired consistency.
2 Pot, seal and label.

Note: For apricot and date chutney, replace the apples with either 400g (1lb) dried apricots which should be soaked overnight in cold water, or 800g (2lb) fresh apricots which should be stoned.

Ingredients

800g (2lb) cooking apples, peeled, cored and sliced
800g (2lb) dates, stoned
200g (8oz) preserved ginger, chopped
400g (1lb) sultanas
400g (1lb) brown sugar
75g (3oz) salt
1 litre (2pt) vinegar

Makes approximately 4kg (8lb)

Green Tomato or Apple Chutney

Method

1 Cook tomatoes, onions, raisins, ginger and bananas in a pan with lid, slowly until tender. If apples are used instead of tomatoes, peel, chop and add 250ml ($\frac{1}{2}$pt) water to prevent burning whilst cooking with the rest of the fruit and vegetables.
2 Add the spices, sugar and vinegar and simmer slowly in the open pan until of a thick consistency.
3 Pot, seal and label.

Ingredients

400g (1lb) green tomatoes or apples roughly chopped
200g (8oz) onions, chopped
200g (8oz) raisins
100g (4oz) preserved ginger, chopped
2 bananas, peeled and sliced
300g (12oz) brown sugar
25g (1oz) salt
1 5ml (tea) spoon cayenne pepper
625ml (1$\frac{1}{4}$pt) vinegar

Makes approximately 1$\frac{1}{2}$kg (3lb)

Marrow Chutney

Method

1 Place marrow into a bowl. Sprinkle liberally with the salt and leave overnight.
2 Drain the marrow well, place into a saucepan with the rest of the ingredients and the peppercorns which should be tied in a small muslin bag.
3 Bring to the boil and simmer until thick with no free liquid.
4 Pot, seal and label.

Ingredients

2kg (4lb) marrow, peeled, deseeded and cubed
salt
200g (8oz) onions, chopped
200g (8oz) cooking apples, peeled, cored and chopped
200g (8oz) sultanas
100g (4oz) brown sugar
750ml (1$\frac{1}{2}$pt) vinegar
1 5ml (tea) spoon ground ginger
12 peppercorns

Makes approximately 1$\frac{1}{2}$kg (3lb)

Automatic Cooking

The automatic control on your cooker can be a real asset if used to the full. It is possible to have a hot cooked meal on the table within minutes of your arriving home. Even breakfast can be cooked automatically just by preparing the dishes and setting the automatic controls the night before.

The oven may be set for delayed stop only. This means that food may be left cooking in the oven, overnight if required, and the oven will switch off at the preset time. This is ideal for the long term cooking of casseroles or a Christmas cake.

In this section we have provided a selection of meals which will help you to become more familiar with automatic cooking.

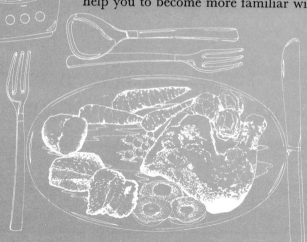

Automatic Meals

Special Points to Remember

1 Check the instructions supplied with the cooker for setting the automatic timer until you are familiar with its operation.

The automatic meals given in this book are for main oven cookery only.

2 Food is placed into the cold oven, so that when planning an automatic meal, add an extra 15 minutes to the normal cooking time to allow for heating the oven. However, the time for the automatic meals given in this book already include the heating up time.

3 Choose dishes which require approximately the same cooking time. Slight variations may be allowed for by
   (a) placing foods in larger or smaller containers,
   (b) using more or less liquid,
   (c) cutting fruit or veg. into larger or smaller pieces.

   These will give longer or shorter cooking times respectively. Further temperature adjustments can be made by placing foods higher or lower in the oven as the top of the oven is slightly hotter than the bottom. This does not apply to fan ovens, where the temperature is even throughout.

4 Arrange shelf positions to suit dishes and choose dishes which will fit into the oven together.

5 As food may be standing for some time in the oven, cover dishes with foil or a lid where possible, and in the case of roast potatoes and joints of meat, brush with a little fat or oil. Lemon juice may be added to fruit to prevent browning.

6 Green leaf vegetables which take only a short time to cook, should not be placed into the oven with the automatic meal. It is far better to cook them in a pan on the hotplate whilst dishing up the rest of the meal.

Lunch-Dinner

1 Chicken, roast potatoes, braised celery, sausage and bacon rolls, apple charlotte

Preparation

1 Prepare sweet corn stuffing.
2 Loosen skin away from the breast of the chicken, fill breast and neck with stuffing. Place any remaining stuffing inside the chicken. Place in roasting tin, on trivet if supplied.
3 Stretch bacon, cut each slice in half lengthwise and twist in a spiral around sausages.
4 Prepare potatoes, toss in oil. Place potatoes and sausages around chicken.
5 Prepare apple charlotte and braised celery, see recipe for method.

Ingredients

sweet corn stuffing (page 72)
1¾kg (3½lb) chicken
sausage and bacon rolls:
200g (8oz) chipolata sausages
4 rashers bacon
1kg (2lb) roast potatoes
apple charlotte (page 88)
braised celery (page 81)

Cooking

Place in the oven as follows:

chicken, roast potatoes, sausages—middle
braised celery, apple charlotte—bottom

Oven temperature: 190–200°C

Time: 1¾ hours

2 Stuffed loin of pork, parsley potatoes, carrots, apple sauce, fruit crumble

Preparation

1 Prepare stuffing, spread over the loin of pork; roll and tie securely; place in a small roasting tin or glass dish.
2 Prepare the potatoes and carrots; place into conveniently sized dishes, (taking into account that they are cooked on the same shelf as the pork); barely cover with salted water; cover with foil. Reserve the parsley to sprinkle over the new potatoes before serving.
3 Prepare fruit crumble (page 86).
4 Place apples in a small ovenware dish and cover with water; cover dish with foil.

Ingredients

sage and onion stuffing (page 72) use half recipe
1½kg (3lb) boned loin of pork
parsley potatoes: 1kg (2lb) new potatoes
parsley, chopped
carrots 600g (1½lb) whole new carrots
fruit crumble (page 86)
apple sauce: 200g (8oz) cooking apples, peeled and sliced

Cooking

Place the meal in the oven as follows:

pork, potatoes, carrots—middle

fruit crumble, apple sauce—bottom

Oven temperature: 190–200°C

Time: 2 hours

3 Moussaka, creme caramel, leeks, peas

Preparation

1 Prepare moussaka (page 65)
2 Prepare leeks and peas; place each into an ovenware dish and barely cover with salted water; cover with foil.
3 Make creme caramel (page 95); place in 4 individual dishes.

Ingredients

moussaka
1kg (2lb) leeks
400g (1lb) peas, frozen
creme caramel

Cooking

Place in the oven as follows:

moussaka, leeks—middle
peas, creme caramel—bottom

Oven temperature: 180–190°C

Time: 1¼ hours

4 Plaice in mushroom sauce, duchesse potatoes, asparagus, mixed vegetables, dutch apple tart

Preparation

1 Prepare plaice in mushroom sauce (page 40)
2 Prepare duchesse potatoes (page 78)
3 Prepare dutch apple tart (page 93)
4 Place the asparagus and the mixed vegetables in ovenware dishes; barely cover with salted water; cover with foil.

Ingredients

plaice in mushroom sauce
duchesse potatoes
dutch apple tart
400g (15oz) tin or 200g (8oz) asparagus, frozen
400g (1lb) mixed vegetables, frozen

Cooking

Place in the oven as follows:

dutch apple tart, mixed vegetables—top
plaice in mushroom sauce, asparagus—middle
duchesse potatoes—bottom

Oven temperature: 210–220°C

Time: 1 hour

5 Hungarian goulash, jacket potatoes, rice pudding, casserole fruit

Preparation

Prepare each of the dishes as described on the appropriate pages

Ingredients

Hungarian goulash (page 61)
baked jacket potatoes (page 78)
rice pudding (page 92)
casserole fruit (page 92)

Cooking

Place the meal in the oven as follows:

goulash, jacket potatoes—top
rice pudding, casserole fruit—middle

Oven temperature: 170–180°C

Time: 2 hours

6 Chicken pie, baked apples, cheesy potatoes, sweet corn

Preparation

1 Prepare chicken pie (page 69)
2 Prepare baked apples (page 86), place on a small baking tray.
3 The cheesy potatoes should be prepared as for duchesse potatoes (page 75). Place half the prepared potato mixture into a conveniently sized shallow ovenware, (taking into account that it is cooked on the same shelf as the apples) sprinkle half the grated cheese over the potato; pipe the rest of the potato on top; sprinkle with remaining cheese.
4 Place sweet corn in a small ovenware dish; barely cover with salted water; cover with foil.

Ingredients

chicken pie
baked apples
cheesy potatoes : 400g (1 lb) potatoes, 50g (2oz) cheese, grated
300g (¾ lb) sweet corn, frozen

Cooking

Place in the oven as follows :

chicken pie, sweet corn —top

cheesy potatoes, baked apples—middle

Oven temperature: 190–200°C

Time: 1 hour

Supper

1 Cornish pasties, chicken pieces, soup, stuffed rolls

Preparation

1 Prepare and cook cornish pasties (page 68), when cool wrap in foil.
2 Roast or grill chicken joints, cool, wrap in foil.
3 Place soup in a shallow ovenware dish, cover with foil.
4 Prepare stuffed rolls (page 18), place on a baking tray.

Ingredients

cornish pasties : 4 medium sized, ready cooked
chicken pieces : 4 chicken joints, ready cooked
soup : 500ml (1pt) prepared soup
stuffed rolls

Cooking

Place in the oven as follows :

cornish pasties, soup— top

chicken pieces, stuffed rolls—bottom

Oven temperature: 190–200°C

Time: 30 minutes

2 Cod in cheese sauce, tomatoes, duchesse potatoes, bakewell tart

Preparation

1 Place cod pieces in a coveniently sized ovenware dish, season, make cheese sauce (page 30), cover the fish.
2 Halve the tomatoes, place on a baking tray, season and knob with butter.
3 Prepare duchesse potatoes (page 78)
4 Make up bakewell tart (page 114)

Ingredients

cod in cheese sauce: 4–6 pieces cod, salt, pepper and lemon juice
500ml (1pt) cheese sauce
4 medium tomatoes
seasoning
knob of butter
duchesse potatoes
bakewell tart

Cooking

Place in the oven as follows:

cod in cheese sauce—top
tomatoes and bakewell tart—middle
duchesse potatoes—bottom

Oven temperature: 170–180°C

Time: 1 hr. 10 minutes

3 Kebabs, cheese cake

Preparation

1 Make cheese cake (page 99).
2 Prepare kebabs (page 55), place on baking tray, brush with oil, cover with foil.
3 Serve kebabs with either rice or french bread.
For rice: place pkt of frozen rice with vegetables in a small ovenware dish, just cover with salted water, cover with foil.
For french bread: Cut french bread into thick slices and wrap in foil.

Ingredients

cheese cake
kebabs
1 pkt frozen rice with vegetables or french bread

Cooking

Place in the oven as follows:

cheese cake—top
kebabs—middle
rice or french bread—bottom

Oven temperature: 170–180°C

Time: 1 hour

Index

Index Continued

Printed in England by Staples Printers Kettering Limited at The George Press, Kettering Northamptonshire   Part No. 2554/961/300